"This is the best book I know for helping readers understand the dynamics of public proclamation. The author's sincere faith and theatrical expertise contribute to a unique book that will help all readers improve something about their ministry, deepen their spiritual lives, and become better persons."

Fr. Paul Turner, pastor,
Cathedral of the Immaculate Conception, Kansas City, MO;
director of the Office of Divine Worship,
Diocese of Kansas City–St. Joseph

"Douglas Leal makes insightful connections between the dynamics of acting and the dynamics of proclaiming Scripture. The result is a fresh approach to the art of proclaiming Scripture that will effectively reach the hearts of listeners, including those who are accustomed to 'changing the channel' when the first few sentences do not stimulate their attention. His book is a gift not only to those who proclaim Scripture, but also to preachers, liturgical presiders, and their mentors."

Rev. Msgr. James A. Mongelluzzo, STD,
professor of liturgy and homiletics, and director of liturgy,
Pope Saint John XXIII National Seminary

"For years I have sought a practical guide to help lectors, deacons, and priests proclaim God's Word. Douglas Leal's *Beyond Reading: Advanced Training for Proclaimers of the Word* is exactly the book I have been waiting for. Grounded in an understanding of oral communication and in years of practice as an actor-teacher, the author presents ten topics that anyone proclaiming the Scripture needs to consider, from preparing the text, to working on aspects of voice and physical presence, to recognizing difficulties in effective proclamation (such as stage fright), to developing a spirituality of living and communicating God's Word. Filled with helpful anecdotes and focused exercises, it even provides an encouraging chapter addressed to those who train lectors. I hope *Beyond Reading* will become a standard reference in parishes and other worshiping communities as well as in lay, diaconal, and priestly programs of formation. It has my highest recommendation."

Fr. Jan Michael Joncas,
artist in residence and research fellow in Catholic studies,
University of St. Thomas, St. Paul, MN

"Douglas Leal does a wonderful job presenting theatre techniques that can help lectors proclaim the Word of God effectively. The aim for lectors is not acting, but reacting to the powerful words of Scripture and giving voice to them in such a way that people can hear that power. This book will be a welcome addition to the formation of lectors."

Maripat Grant, coordinator,
Office of Worship, Diocese of Erie;
liturgy director, St. Mark the Evangelist Parish, Erie, PA

"Accessible, inviting, and theologically coherent, this book provides effective techniques for enabling lectors to convey to the faithful the life already present in the Scriptures. Douglas Leal's clear, engaging prose conveys his conviction, rooted in long experience, that the resources of the acting profession can help turn ordinary readers into proclaimers of the Word. Good stories and particularly fitting examples from Scripture illumine his well-organized and helpful ideas and exercises."

Fr. Charles Gordon, csc,
codirector of the Garaventa Center for
Catholic Intellectual Life and American Culture,
University of Portland

"This reworking of Douglas Leal's original book earns a standing ovation from me. The best of the original work is enhanced and extended by this innovative new edition. His advice on emotion and intention has transformed my teaching in the seminary and parishes where I minister. Inspired by him, our seminary nurtures passionate proclaimers who are truly people of the Word. We are blessed by his work, wisdom, and love of Scripture that shine through so well in this book, and we are deeply grateful."

Anne Frawley-Mangan,
Holy Spirit Seminary,
Brisbane, Australia, and Litmus Productions

"This is a must-read book for lay proclaimers of the Word, but I would also encourage all clergy persons to read this excellent text. In fact, all who love Scripture would benefit from the author's insights. The goal of the book is to help those who proclaim Scripture at Mass bring the sacred texts alive for the those who hear them. Douglas Leal's masterful skills as an instructor and coach will be deeply appreciated by all of us who have been given the sacred responsibility of making God present in the proclaimed Word."

Fr. John Cusick, Archdiocese of Chicago

BEYOND READING

Advanced Training for Proclaimers
of the Word of God

DOUGLAS LEAL

LTP

LITURGY
TRAINING
PUBLICATIONS

Nihil Obstat
Rev. Mr. Daniel G. Welter, JD
Chancellor
Archdiocese of Chicago
October 5, 2020

Imprimatur
Most Rev. Robert G. Casey
Vicar General
Archdiocese of Chicago
October 5, 2020

In memory of my mother, who first taught me to read,
and for my sister, Susan,
who continues to encourage me to proclaim

CONTENTS

ACKNOWLEDGMENTS

This book probably would not exist without the vision of two people: Helen Nicole St. Paul, the editor of the first edition, who saw my experience in acting and in liturgy and thought we might get a useful book out of it, and Lorie Simmons, who shepherded the creation of this edition. Most of what ended up here I learned from the many talented people with whom I've worked over the years as an actor and director, and I'm very grateful for their guidance and collaboration. I especially want to thank Joey Marino, Pamela Salem, Dave McAdam, Kelly Ford, Carla Taravella, and Anne Frawley-Mangan, colleagues who helped me clarify the presentation of these ideas. Finally, heartfelt thanks to all my friends and family who encouraged me, prodded me, and prayed for me during this process. Any wisdom in this book belongs rightly to the Spirit; any errors are my own.

The Sacred Art of Acting and the Sacred Act of Proclaiming

We must look for good readers! Those who know how to read, not those who read "meh, meh, meh, meh" and nothing is understood. Good readers. They must be prepared and rehearse before the Mass in order to read well.

—Francis, General Audience, January 31, 2018

This call for "good readers" is echoed each week in communities all over the world. We long to be fed with God's Word, proclaimed so that our hearts can receive the fullness of life it contains. By your interest in this book, you're responding to that call, so, on behalf of all those who hunger, let me start by saying, "Thank you!" I think what I offer in these pages will be of great use to you as you bring this gift to your community.

You may be new to the ministry of proclaiming and looking for advice beyond your basic training. Or perhaps you've been a lector for years and want to refine and improve your skills. If you train proclaimers, you may be seeking a new perspective on guiding those you train. Or you may be a pastor or deacon looking to improve your proclamation and preaching skills. I hope to put my experience and training at your service.

First, though, let me clarify the terms used for this ministry. In common usage, lay proclaimers of the Word in Catholic parishes are called either *lectors* or *readers*.[1] In this book, I use the terms *reader, lector,* and *proclaimer* interchangeably.

The book is designed for anyone who proclaims Scripture in any religious tradition. I am a Catholic Christian, and this book reflects my familiarity with that tradition, but what I've outlined here should be helpful to those in other traditions as well, especially liturgical traditions and other Christian churches that use a lectionary. Even those from non-Christian traditions in which sacred texts are read aloud will benefit from these skills.

My focus in this book is on helping you grasp your role as a sacred storyteller and on sharing practical techniques you can use right away to improve your proclamation. That's because proclaiming is not solely an intellectual exercise, but requires practical, physical skill. The only way you learn such a skill is by learning technique and practicing what you learn. Thus, this book is full of exercises that will help you connect the Word you proclaim, not just with your mind and your spirit, but with your voice and your body and, ultimately, with your community. This book is mostly about doing because the ministry of proclaiming is an active ministry.

Of course, it's important to understand the context in which you minister as well. As a sacred storyteller in a specific tradition, your understanding of

---

1. Technically speaking, an "instituted lector" is a lay reader who has been "instituted" in a liturgical ceremony celebrated by an ordinary (a bishop). Here in North America, parishes are served by many lay readers who have been trained and often commissioned, but there are very few instituted lectors.

both the story and the tradition is essential to your ministry. I encourage you to learn all you can about the theological background of liturgy and Scripture from the many excellent resources available. (See the Helpful Resources listed on pages 134–135.) In turn, this book will help you integrate your liturgical and scriptural knowledge with the practical skills of proclaiming.

To coach you in the techniques and methods most useful for developing these skills, I've drawn on my experience working as one who proclaims publicly in another medium: the actor. I've worked as an actor for about as long as I've been a lector. And I've worked as a director in a variety of theaters: high school, college, community theater, and professional. In all this work, I've found the techniques I share in this book to be the most useful, not only to my work as an actor, but also to my ministry as a proclaimer.

The Sacred Art of Acting

That's not surprising. An actor's job is similar to a lector's. An actor is presented with a text—words on a page—and out of that text must create a life before an audience. A lector is also presented with a text, but a text that already has a life within it. The lector does not create a life, but rather connects with the life that's there and expresses it in the midst of the community.

The relationship between the two vocations is not a coincidence. The art of acting grew out of ancient religious celebrations in Egypt, Greece, and elsewhere, and actors were once considered sacred ministers. In some cultures still, the spiritual leaders are those who can embody and proclaim the spiritual wisdom of the culture and the prayers and needs of the community itself.

Actors who really understand their craft know that they carry on this sacred tradition. An actor's job is "to hold as 'twer the Mirrour up to Nature," as Hamlet says,[2] so that those in the audience can see themselves in it—their true faults and foibles as well as their praiseworthy traits. A lector's job is also to hold up a mirror. But in this mirror we see ourselves not only as we are—we see ourselves as we are called to be. The mirror of Scripture reflects our relationship with God and how God calls us to be in that relationship and in our relationships with others and all of creation.

It's very important that, before we begin, we know where we want to end. The athlete must know where the finish line is; the pianist must know how the sonata should sound. As you might have guessed from the title of this book, I want to coach you in the skills you need, not merely to read well, but to proclaim fully the Scripture you're given. Our goal is *proclamation*. Now, you might ask, what's the difference between reading and proclaiming? What does it mean to proclaim? Why is reading alone insufficient? Well, I'm glad you asked!

---

2. *Hamlet,* act 3, scene 2.

The Sacred Act of Proclaiming

In 2004, John Paul II reflected that although Roman Catholics can now hear the Scripture at liturgy in their own language, rather than in Latin, something is still often lacking. "It is not enough that the biblical passages are read in the vernacular, if they are not also proclaimed with the care, preparation, devout attention and meditative silence that enable the word of God to touch people's minds and hearts."[3]

To touch minds and hearts, it is the *Word of God* that must be proclaimed, not just the words, and there is a distinction. The words of Scripture are an assemblage of letters organized into sentences, verses, paragraphs, and chapters. When read clearly, they have meaning, yes, but little else. The *Word of God* starts with those same words but also encompasses the energy, emotion, life, intent, dreams, prayers, struggles, joys, cries, hopes, and, most of all, love that is found within those words. That is what we are called to proclaim, and that is the difference between reading and proclaiming. In proclamation, Francis tells us, "the pages of the Bible cease to be writings and become living words, spoken by God."[4]

When Paul says that he "proclaimed" the Gospel to the Romans (15:20; 16:25), the Corinthians (1 Corinthians 1:23), the Colossians (1:28), and others, he doesn't mean he came to those cities and just spoke words to them. He means that he showed them, with his life and with his teaching, by his attitude and by his example, all that the Gospel of Jesus Christ contains. Of course, Jesus himself was a proclaimer in the same way. When he proclaimed the reign of God, he did so with his life more than with his words. His wordless moments—eating with sinners, healing the suffering, touching the outcasts, and, most especially, his death and resurrection—proclaimed more about the reign of God and discipleship than all his teachings, important though they are.

We know that worship is much more than just saying the right words. The first document of the Second Vatican Council, *Sacrosanctum concilium*, revived the early Christian understanding of liturgy as a "work of the people" (which is what the word *liturgy* means). It reminded us that full, active, and conscious participation is the "right and duty" of the faithful "by reason of their baptism."[5] Without that participation, the liturgy is valid, but it is hardly the worship experience we are called to. You know this yourself. You know when liturgies envelop you in their life and infuse themselves into your life, they stay with you and sustain you through the week. Those liturgies are the source and summit of your spiritual life. At other times, although all the same words are spoken, the liturgy seems to hide the life it contains.

But, some may protest, the words we are called to read aren't just any words. If we simply read them well, won't their power still be felt? After all, the Word

---

3. *Mane nobiscum Domine*, 13.
4. General Audience, January 31, 2018.
5. *Sacrosanctum concilium*, 14.

we read is sharper than a two-edged sword; it does what it says; it does not return unfulfilled (Hebrews 4:12; Isaiah 55:11). True, and this is exactly why reading is insufficient. To simply read the words, even to read them clearly, and ignore the life that is within those words, is to be unfaithful to the ministry of lector or Gospel proclaimer. If, rather than working on really proclaiming, we simply read and expect the power of the Word to do the rest, we are like the servant who buried his master's money in the ground for fear of losing it (Matthew 25:14–30). We are expected to make a return on the investment we've been given, and making that return requires us to take the risk of proclamation.

Suppose translators shared this attitude that the power of the Word overcomes any defect in interpretation. These scholars labor intensely over which word or turn of phrase most completely conveys the meaning of the text in the original language. But suppose these scholars were to say, "Well, the Word of God is alive already. What does it really matter if we work to find just the right way to translate it? The power of the Word is not diminished by a poor translation." Perhaps, but then that power is not available to those who will read it.

Proclaimers are translators as well. We translate the written Word of God to the spoken Word or, more accurately, to the proclaimed Word. If we rest on the assumption that the Word is so powerful we needn't proclaim it fully—with all the effort and energy we put into telling the most important stories of our own lives—then we present a poor translation that keeps the power of the Word from being revealed to our community.

You can see now, I hope, why proclamation, more than reading, is required from us as ministers of the Word. You might also be able to see why we can learn how to proclaim by borrowing some techniques, methods, and tips from actors. Yet you may still be cautious. You may have heard or been told, for example, that lectors must take care not to go "over the top" in their reading or become too theatrical, that lectors are not to attempt to interpret the Scripture they read. A lector trainer once told me, "I make sure to tell all my lectors, 'Reading is not a performance!' The focus should be on the Word and not on the lector." I agree.

But isn't that what happens in the best performances? Aren't the performances of our most talented actors successful because they lose themselves in the characters they portray, so we focus on the story and not on the actor? Throughout this book, I will help you bring real vigor to your proclamation without going over the top. I'll caution you about any dangers of turning a reading into a performance. I've devoted a whole chapter to this, in fact. In turn, I'll ask you to be willing to take a risk, to go a bit further than you may initially be comfortable going, to really get a return on your proclamation rather than burying it safely in a "reading." Remember, we are not called to be a timid people! "God did not give us a spirit of timidity, but the Spirit of power and love and self-control" (2 Timothy 1:7, New Jerusalem Bible). Which is the more frequent experience: hearing Scripture read as if it were an instruction manual for a power tool, or hearing a bold, expressive proclamation? Don't we owe it to our communities to step out in faith and *proclaim*?

This may seem daunting at first. It isn't—it is serious, it is important, but it is also doable, and it's my hope to show you, with the help of the Spirit of power and love and self-control, how to do it.

How to Use This Book

This book summarizes ten skills that I think a proclaimer can learn from an actor and that are foundational to both callings. The chapters in the book are arranged in a skill-building format so that the skills developed in early chapters form the foundation for work in later chapters. However, the skills are also complete in themselves so that your proclamation should benefit from your learning even the most basic ones. Chapter 1 examines storytelling and its relationship to the ministry of the proclaimer. Chapters 2, 3, and 4 introduce some of the foundational, technical skills on text, voice, and physicalization. Chapters 5, 6, and 7 address intention and emotion, the elements that underpin real proclamation. The last three chapters give some advice on handling stage fright, reading cold (and with a cold), preparing well, and, most important, living the Word you proclaim.

For this edition, I've included two additional chapters—chapter 11 with suggestions for proclaiming texts other than readings (such as prayers of intercession), and chapter 12 with advice for those who train lectors. Finally, I have included a form for giving feedback on a proclamation and a list of helpful resources.

There are a lot of techniques and exercises given in these pages. You may be overwhelmed by their number and detail. Don't be concerned. I've presented a variety of techniques because everyone is different. Some techniques you will find easy; some will be difficult even after much trial. Some may never seem to work for you. It's the same for actors. While some actors are fervent disciples of a particular teacher or method, others do very well working with different techniques or a mix. I encourage you to try each suggestion a few times before deciding it doesn't work for you. To help you sort it all out, I've summarized the important points at the conclusion of each chapter.

Throughout the book, I've included summary boxes and icons to help alert you to specific types of information.

 Look for the scroll and quill icon to alert you to important details you may want to "take note" of.

 Each chapter also includes a few tools from the "Actor's Toolbox," which give pointers on specific situations, trouble spots, or advanced techniques that are supplemental to the main point of the chapter.

 I've also pointed out some potential traps—pitfalls to be cautious about or things that could lead you astray represented by a ballet slipper in a trap.

In fact, the first trap I want to point out is that, if you're an experienced lector, you may be tempted to skip some of the basic skill work covered in the first few chapters. I advise against this. Conscientious artists and athletes are always honing even their most basic techniques. Likewise, as you advance through the skills, you'll find that returning to work on an earlier chapter will yield even more results.

It might take you several months or more to work through all the techniques in this book, especially if you have few opportunities to proclaim. Don't worry, and don't rush. As you incorporate each skill into your ministry, it should start bearing fruit for you right away. Even after you go through all the chapters, you'll find it useful to come back to this book from time to time for a "tune-up." Proclaimers, like actors and other artists, can pick up bad habits along the way or become lazy about certain skills, so it's always good to check back in and make sure you're still paying attention to the important elements.

A word about texts. Except where noted, all Scripture quotations come from the United States Roman Catholic *Lectionary for Mass*. Longer excerpts from the lectionary are identified both with their Scripture citation and the Sunday and year (A, B, C—the first, second, or third year in the three-year cycle of readings), from which the excerpt is taken. For example, 5 Lent C would indicate the Fifth Sunday of Lent, Year C; Ordinary 23B would refer to the Twenty-Third Sunday in Ordinary Time, Year B. (Chapter 2 explains how the lectionary is organized.) Communities that use the *Revised Common Lectionary* have a different designation for Sundays in Ordinary Time, which is given in a footnote: *Epiphany* designates Sundays after Epiphany and *Proper* indicates Sundays after Pentecost. Note that the examples given are often *excerpts* from the readings rather than the complete readings. Occasionally I have quoted from the Introduction to the *Lectionary for Mass*. The Introduction provides valuable information about the role of Scripture in the Mass, the role and training of the lector, the rationale behind the selection of Scripture in the lectionary, and the way it is organized. Scripture quotations from the *New Revised Standard Version* are noted as NRSV, and quotations from *The New Jerusalem Bible* as NJB.

I hope you'll find this work both stimulating and fun. I've tried to keep things light and engaging. Both for fun and by way of illustration, I've included some "Behind the Scenes" anecdotes about the world of acting, highlighted by this "Behind the Scenes" icon. The work of proclamation does have its lighter moments. Consider this: Do you think Jesus had fun as he told stories? Did he enjoy relating the pompous prayer of the upright man in the temple (Luke 18:9–14) or the weariness of the judge pestered by the importunate widow (Luke 18:1–7)? He must have, since he did it so often, and he surely knew that humor imparts wisdom. His example can inspire us to see the human comedy in our ministry as well. Our task is an awesome one, but also an enjoyable one. In fact, such enjoyment is a sign that we've been called to the right ministry.

Now let's begin!

Take Note

Actor's Toolbox

Traps

Behind the Scenes

Chapter 1

Working on Storytelling: Be Passionate or Stay Home

Barry Levinson's film *Avalon* opens on a family gathered together for Thanksgiving dinner in 1948. Sam is telling his grandchildren and grand-nieces and -nephews the story of how he and his brothers immigrated to America. He tells how, as each brother arrived, he worked hard to make enough money to bring the next one over, until the entire family, including their father, was settled in America. He tells how they met the girls who would become their wives, how they married, lived, and in some cases died. As he shares the story, his wife calls them in for dinner. She complains that she's tired of hearing the story. The children already know it; he's told it many times before. But Sam protests: The story must be told and retold because when you stop remembering, you forget.

What Levinson has depicted in this scene beautifully parallels the Eucharistic liturgy. Like Sam's family, we gather together each Sunday around a table of thanksgiving. And before we share the meal, we listen to the story— our story—the story of our family: how we came to be, who our mothers and fathers were, how they lived, what they stood for, how they died. Our remembering them makes them present again. There's a Hebrew word for this act of remembrance, *zikkaron*; the concept underpins not only the Eucharist but also most of the celebrations and liturgies in the Jewish calendar.[1]

We make present again, especially in the Eucharist, but also in the Word, the Christ at the center of our community. The primary act of remembrance is, of course, the Eucharistic meal. We follow Jesus' command to "Do this in memory of me." But the meal we receive from the table of the Word is a complement to the meal we receive from the table of the Eucharist.[2] We gather together not only to celebrate a meal but to reconnect with who we are, and knowing who we are requires knowing where we come from, and knowing where we come from requires someone to tell our story.

The History of Our Story

The story we inherit stretches back to that day, many millennia ago, when someone rose up in the midst of their gathered tribe and began to tell the first story. Maybe the story told of the location of water, or food, or shelter. Maybe

---

1. The analogous term used by Christian liturgists is a Greek word: *anamnesis*.

2. "The church has always venerated the divine scriptures as it has venerated the Body of the Lord, in that it never ceases, above all in the sacred liturgy, to partake of the bread of life and to offer it to the faithful from the one table of the word of God and the Body of Christ." *Dei Verbum*, 21.

it warned of danger. In any case, it may have been the first instance of language moving beyond "I want" or "Do this" or "Run away" to telling about the past or the future.

Many stories were told and retold, but the ones that were kept the longest, the ones that really meant something, were the important stories: the stories of how things came to be the way they are, the stories of how people should act to preserve life and preserve the group, the stories of the ancestors who defined the group. Someone told the story of how the tribe came to be, what their identity was, what gave them their "us-ness" and what gave others their "them-ness."

As stories passed from generation to generation, events that were deemed less important were dropped, and other details were added that seemed more important to the storyteller. As they passed through the years, the most important stories were the ones that stuck.

This is how we inherited our story in the form of Scripture. Before being written, most of Scripture started as oral stories. Some—the stories of Genesis and Exodus, for example—were passed down many generations and went through much editing before being recorded. Others, such as the Gospels and epistles, were recorded fairly soon after they began. As the oral tradition was passed along, and even after the stories were written, they were edited so that only the most important remained. Consider the Gospels: Jesus was in public ministry for three years, and yet the Gospels record, in total, no more than a few weeks. Why were the stories culled to the few that remain? Why, from all the stories that were available to them, did the writers of sacred Scripture choose to include the events they did? Because they, under the guidance of the Holy Spirit, deemed that these events were the important ones; these were the stories worth telling; these were the stories about *the day something happened.*

Imagine an episode of your favorite show in which you are shown the ordinary, everyday lives of the characters. They go about their business of eating, working, playing, and maybe even watching their favorite show. It would be a pretty uninteresting episode which few people, I suspect, would watch for very long. No one's mother-in-law would be coming to visit; no romance might be about to break up; no crime would need to be solved. There's a reason why, when someone's life is full of incident, we call it "drama." Plays, screenplays, and television scripts are written about the day something happened.

This is also what we tell in our stories. Sam tells his grandchildren about the significant events in his life. He doesn't say, "One day in 1922, I woke up, went to work, came home, and went to sleep." His grandchildren would soon find something else to do!

 From the Bible, a further selection has been made to create a lectionary. The Christian churches that use a lectionary have decided that, out of all the important stories that ended up in Scripture, the stories we hear on Sundays are the "more important" and "more significant" ones.[3] What we read on Sundays and feast days then, are the really, *really* important stories of our faith.

The Storyteller

A story needs a storyteller.

The need for storytelling is not so obvious in our culture today, but when people lived in cultures with an oral tradition, storytelling was vital. It was integral to maintaining the identity of the group and to preserving their traditions and taboos. The telling of the stories was limited to special members, people set apart, people who devoted time to the learning and telling these stories. Because the stories were sacred, the storytellers were sacred, too.

Once writing developed in a culture, some very prescient individuals decided that the stories should be written down. As with every advance in technology, much was gained, but some things were lost. The written word allowed the story to be preserved, relatively unchanged; it allowed the story to be disseminated farther than the oral tradition. But with the written word came the slow death of the storyteller. The storyteller wasn't needed to preserve the stories; they were already preserved. The storyteller wasn't needed to gather the group together, as the stories could be read by individuals, at least those who could read. For those who could not, the stories were read aloud by a reader, but a reader is not a storyteller.

This is the situation we find ourselves in today, and it's partially responsible for the confusion between reading and proclamation that I discussed in the introduction. If we live in a literate society, then why do we need a storyteller? Why don't we just read the stories for ourselves?

When we hear the story from a storyteller in the midst of our community, we connect with the story and the community in a way that is impossible when we read it for ourselves. We listen to the story and we watch the story on the face of the teller (notice we don't read along with a storyteller), so that the life of the story is made available to us again. And we do so in the midst of our community, not in the isolation of our room with a Bible in our lap, important though private Bible-reading is to our spiritual life. Writing about the connection between liturgy and community, Henri Nouwen says, "When we listen to the word [as a community], we not only receive insight into God's saving work, but we also experience a new mutual bond."[4] As Christians, we understand that the fullest expression of the life of Christ comes to us through community. I, alone, am not the Body of Christ; we, the community, are the Body of Christ. And for the community as a whole to experience the story, we still need a storyteller.

The writer Walter Wangerin gives the following charge to parents who tell the Christmas story to their children.

---

3. "Sundays and festive days present the more important biblical passages. In this way the more significant parts of God's revealed word can be read to the assembled faithful within an appropriate period of time." Introduction, *Lectionary for Mass*, 65.

4. Henri J. M. Nouwen, *Reaching Out: The Three Movements of the Spiritual Life* (New York: Image Books, 1975), 156–157.

When you speak of loving, seem to love. Describing sorrow, be sad. Let fear come through a harried voice, and gladness come with laughter, and triumph sound like exultation. Half of the life of the story is the story's teller. Your voice and face and body give it form. It is you whom the children see and hear. They will not distinguish. It is you who will love or not, and so the story will or will not love.[5]

Half of the life of the story is the story's teller. The story left on the page is incomplete. The story needs a teller. In this passage, Wangerin has written a mission statement for the lector-storyteller.

Wordplay

Do you remember *onomatopoeia* from your high school English class? The term refers to words that sound like what they mean: *pop, tinkle, splash, growl,* and so on. When we read these words aloud, they become like the sound-effects track in a movie; they enliven our story and set the mood in our listeners' imaginations.

While Scripture contains few truly onomatopoetic words, there are occasions when we can choose to sound words in a way that gives a similar effect. Consider the line "How I long for all of you with the affection of Christ Jesus" (Philippians 1:8b). We can convey Paul's longing by elongating our pronunciation of *long,* by making the word sound like what it conveys.

There are many such opportunities in the Scriptures. Here are a few more examples:

[Jesus] *rebuked* them

and directed them not to tell this to anyone. (Luke 9:21)

We don't have the words of Jesus' rebuke, but if we say the word *rebuked* sharply, we convey the feeling.

Then they *spat* in his face and *struck* him,

while some *slapped* him. (Matthew 26:67)

We can hit these words hard to convey the violence they describe.

Then will the lame *leap* like a stag,

then the tongue of the mute will *sing.*

Streams will *burst forth* in the desert,

and rivers in the steppe. (Isaiah 35:6)

Raise your voice on *leap* to convey the idea of height; elongate *sing* to make the word sound musical; put some power behind *burst forth.*

Look at your proclamation for more of these kinds of words, and have some fun with them!

To be the kind of storyteller Wangerin describes, we need three things: knowledge of the story, skills in its telling, and passion.

1. Knowledge of the story comes from our study of Scripture. We are tellers of the story first, and students of the story second. While it's not true that every music history professor is a skilled musician, it is true that the best

---

5. "The Christmas Story," in *The Manger Is Empty: Stories in Time* (San Francisco: Harper and Row, 1989), 27.

Beyond Reading: Advanced Training for Proclaimers of the Word of God

musicians know their music history, and this knowledge informs their playing. It's the same with our study of Scripture; it's not our primary focus, but it needs to be an important part of our formation.

2. For skill development, well, that's what this book is for. The exercises herein, along with assiduous practice, should help you develop the skills you need to be Wangerin's kind of storyteller.

3. The one thing remaining, then, is passion, and that is perhaps the one thing most needed. It is also, unfortunately, the one thing that can't be taught.

Passion

It's the same for actors. Acting is a very hard pursuit to make into a profession. Hundreds if not thousands of would-be actors descend on Los Angeles, New York, Chicago, London, Sydney, Vancouver, and other places every year to try their hand. Acting requires no professional training; there's no certification program or state licensing board; there's not even an agreed-on standard that determines whether anyone is "good" at acting. The number of pop stars, athletes, politicians, and the like who end up acting seems to prove that "anyone can do it." And, of course, as in most fields, much of the work goes to people who may be new but are still "connected"—those with parents, relatives, or friends already in the industry. Faced with such a reality, actors who aren't really passionate about pursuing this work would be far better off spending their time and energy on other things. The only people willing to put up with such formidable odds are those who feel called: those who are unfulfilled doing anything but acting.

Passion is also required for storytelling. If these are our most important stories, if these are the stories about the day something happened, then, above all, these are the stories that require passion. Look at the passion inherent in the early stories of our faith. Look at the passion used to tell these stories over the centuries.

There was so much passion, even in the telling of the law, that the people wept on hearing it after returning from exile (Nehemiah 8). Look at the passion of the prophets telling of God's great love for Israel. Imagine the storytellers of the first Christian century, rising in the gathered community to tell the story of how Jesus forgave sinners, or cured a paralytic, or died and rose from the dead. These stories must have been told with great passion, especially knowing that the act of telling them could cost the tellers their lives!

We inherit this legacy of words, a wealth untold: words that emboldened the community, strengthened them in time of siege, healed them in time of grief, challenged them in time of complacency, exhorted them when they flagged, cheered them when they succeeded, and soothed them when they sorrowed. These are words filled with passion, and they need to be told with passion by those who, like struggling actors and artists, are called to do it.

Now maybe you don't feel called to be a lector-storyteller. Maybe you didn't volunteer; maybe you were asked or were "volunteered" by someone else. (If so, you're in good company, as that's how the disciples were called. Jesus didn't hold sign-ups in the synagogue courtyard after Sabbath services. He said, "You— follow me!") But I suspect that you have been called simply because you're reading this book right now. If you've picked up this book and you're willing to put time and energy into improving your skills, then you've been called!

If you're still not sure, then I suggest you work through this book and see how you feel. The exercises may fit you like an old pair of jeans, a sign that your gifts are made for this ministry. If, though, you struggle endlessly with this, if nothing seems to work, not this book nor anything else you try to improve your skills, then perhaps this ministry doesn't fit your gifts. That's good to know, too, because it means somewhere there's a ministry that fits you well but isn't getting done because you're not there to do it yet. Go and find that ministry as fast as you can!

 When successful actors are asked by an interviewer to give advice to actors just starting out, they inevitably come up with one of two responses. One is something along the lines of "Never give up on your dream. Keep working hard, and it will be worth it." The other is "The minute you find something else you enjoy doing, do it." The responses seem like contradictions, but they are actually two ways of expressing the same basic message: "Be passionate, or go home."

My suspicion is that you'll fall somewhere between these two extremes. The ministry will be work; some of the exercises will be easy, some hard, but you'll also feel rewarded and fulfilled as you do it. This is a sign that you are called and, I hope, a sign of your passion for this work.

Our Model Storyteller

Wangerin gives us a great definition of the storyteller, but for a model, there's no one better than Jesus himself. Jesus was a consummate storyteller; he taught by telling stories. And he must have been good at it because he had crowds of listeners: Everyone was amazed and spellbound at his "gracious words," which had authority and impact (Mark 1:22; Luke 4:22; Luke 19:48).

Too bad we can't watch Jesus tell his stories. I bet we could learn a great deal. But we can take advantage of learning from the storytellers we already know. Over the next week or month, pay attention to people as they tell stories, especially as they tell ones they are passionate about: stories of their grandchildren, their favorite sports teams, movies they loved. Be a student of storytelling. Observe how a story appears in the teller's face and body. Listen to how the story changes in the voice. Look at the intensity and focus in the eyes. See the teller's need to communicate and how emotions are expressed during the telling of the story.

Now, here's a little secret. If you watch the best storytellers closely enough and can translate what they do into your proclamations, you don't need to work through the rest of this book! If, however, you want to know more specifically how you can bring that same passion to the story you proclaim, then let's continue.

Four Important Things to Remember about Storytelling:

1. The stories of Scripture, especially the ones we read during worship, are the most important of all the stories in our tradition. They are the stories about the day something happened.

2. Half of the life of the story is the teller.

3. Lectors are storytellers. A storyteller needs
   - ✤ knowledge of the story
   - ✤ skills to tell the story
   - ✤ passion in the telling

4. Take advantage of opportunities and resources to learn more about Scripture, liturgy, and storytelling.

Chapter 2

Working on Preparing the Text: It's All in the Text

Text work is the first job for every proclaimer. For a proclamation to be effective, proclaimers must know what they are saying, and this knowledge comes only from a study of the text.

Know the Source

It's very important, as I will emphasize a number of times, for the proclaimer to be a student of Scripture.

Lectors should avail themselves of every opportunity to learn more about Scripture and should build a collection of useful tools—books, websites, articles— that will help them in their study. (A good study Bible with numerous footnotes, essays, and other reference material is the first, best resource for a lector.) Perhaps your knowledge of Scripture is already advanced. If not, it will be helpful as we continue our work for you to have at least a basic understanding of the contents of the various books of the Bible. A very simple summary, then, follows. (Much more nuanced divisions are possible.) You might want to refer back to this as you progress through the rest of this work.

Old Testament

- The Pentateuch: Genesis, Exodus, Leviticus, Numbers, Deuteronomy— These five books (which is what the word *pentateuch* means) relate how the world and its peoples came to be, especially the people of Israel and their identity as God's chosen people. Many of the best-known Bible stories are in these books: the Garden of Eden, Abraham and Isaac, Noah's ark, Joseph, Moses, the escape from Egypt, the Ten Commandments. These books comprise the Torah, the central text of the Jewish faith.
- History books: Joshua, Judges, Ruth, 1 and 2 Samuel, 1 and 2 Kings, 1 and 2 Chronicles, Ezra, Nehemiah, Tobit, Judith, Esther, 1 and 2 Maccabees— As the name of this category implies, these books relate the early history of the nation of Israel and the Israelites' relationship with God. The stories of Joshua, David, Solomon, and Elijah are in these books.
- Wisdom books: Job, Psalms, Proverbs, Ecclesiastes, Song of Songs, Wisdom, Sirach — These books teach the ways of the wise and the virtues of wisdom. The Book of Psalms is essentially the Jewish hymnal.
- Prophets: Isaiah, Jeremiah, Lamentations, Baruch, Ezekiel, Daniel, Hosea, Joel, Amos, Obadiah, Jonah, Micah, Nahum, Habakkuk, Zephaniah,

Haggai, Zechariah, Malachi—These books form a record of the prophets' preaching to Israel, especially in times of crisis, and demonstrate the unwavering faithfulness of God despite the struggles of the nation to remain faithful. The books also contain the prophecies about God's ultimate plan of salvation, the Messiah, which Christians see fulfilled in Jesus.

New Testament

⊕ Gospels: Matthew, Mark, Luke, John—The stories of the life and ministry of Jesus. Matthew, Mark, and Luke record very similar events. If placed side by side, the same story might be viewed in all three "with one glance"; thus, they are called the *synoptic* Gospels, from the Greek word for "at a glance."

⊕ Acts of the Apostles—From the author of Luke, an account of the development of the early Christian community.

⊕ Paul's letters (epistles): Romans, 1 and 2 Corinthians, Galatians, Ephesians, Philippians, Colossians, 1 and 2 Thessalonians, 1 and 2 Timothy, Titus, Philemon— The earliest writings in the New Testament, these letters record the teachings of Paul and the first developments in Christian theology.

⊕ Other letters: Hebrews; James; 1 and 2 Peter; 1, 2, and 3 John; Jude—More teachings from writers other than Paul. They are sometimes called the *catholic letters* because they are written to the universal (catholic) church instead of a particular community.

⊕ Revelation—This book is written in a specific style known as *apocalyptic* writing; its main message is that no matter what the conflict, God will prevail in the end.

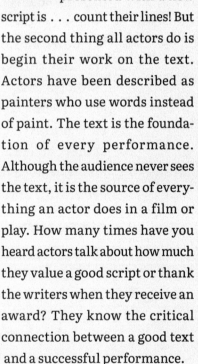

The first thing all actors do when they are presented with a new script is . . . count their lines! But the second thing all actors do is begin their work on the text. Actors have been described as painters who use words instead of paint. The text is the foundation of every performance. Although the audience never sees the text, it is the source of everything an actor does in a film or play. How many times have you heard actors talk about how much they value a good script or thank the writers when they receive an award? They know the critical connection between a good text and a successful performance.

The rest of this chapter gives a number of ways to work closely with the text as you prepare your proclamation. As with all the techniques in this book, you will undoubtedly find some more helpful than others. Try each one at least a few times, and stick with the ones that work best for you.

If you're having difficulty with a particular text, come back and try one of the techniques you don't usually use. It may be just the key you need to unlock the problem passage.

As you begin your work with the text—and as you continue through the rest of these chapters—you'll find it very useful to have a copy of your reading that you can mark up, just as a musician marks a piece of music. Best of all is a copy that matches the text layout of the copy you'll actually be proclaiming from.

You may want to make additional copies so you can mark up as much as you need and still have a clean copy to work from when needed. If you don't have an exact copy of the text as it appears in the lectionary, be aware that you can't simply take the text from Scripture, even if you have the same translation. In the lectionary, you'll find slight modifications to the Bible text to improve clarity—added introductory or explanatory phrases, some changes in language, or reordering of words. Always get an exact copy of the text, if not the exact layout, as it appears in the lectionary from which you'll proclaim.

Read the Text Through Completely First

Constanin Stanislavski, a Russian actor from early last century whose ideas about acting continue to have a profound influence on theater and film, said that the first reading of a script is a unique opportunity that actors must approach with care. Never again will the actor read the script as an uninformed newcomer. Only in the first reading will the actor be surprised by an unexpected revelation in the story or be in suspense about how the play ends. Only in that first reading, in fact, will the actor experience the story the same way the audience will: with no preconceived notions, expectations, or knowledge.

The same, of course, cannot be said about the texts of Scripture. We know these stories; some of them we know very well. Still, there is value in taking special care during your first reading of a text as you prepare for proclamation. Thus, when you are first assigned a reading, don't immediately rush to read it. Rather, wait until you can give it the time it deserves. When you sit down to read it, do so slowly and carefully. Put yourself in the mind of someone who has never heard the story before. Read it all the way through in one sitting.

When you've finished this reading, record some of your first impressions: What is the reading about? What feeling or feelings do I get from it? What words or phrases strike me? What seems to be missing? What didn't I understand? You'll be amazed that, even though you will go far deeper and do far more work with the text as you prepare, some of your initial impressions will be the most valid.

Read it over again a few times, all the way through, before you start some of the work outlined in the rest of this book. You will soon be delving deeply into the text, but before you do, you'll want to spend a little more time just reading it without thinking about the work ahead. This will help you get the whole picture of the passage before you begin breaking it apart for your work.

Check the Dictionary

In addition to a study Bible, every lector needs a good dictionary—not just a Bible dictionary but a standard dictionary or an authoritative online dictionary.

Do you know that *vindication* doesn't mean the same as *vengeance*? Do you know the difference between *rejoice* and *exult*? Do you know the meaning of *recompense, festal, winnow, couch, clamorous, reprove*? Are you sure? Are you really sure? It's always helpful to look up words, even those you're confident you know, to understand fully the nuances of meaning. Look it up!

Identify the Style

Our first real work with the text comes in determining the style.

There are a number of different ways to classify the styles of Scripture texts. I've outlined a classification that will be most helpful for proclaimers. This is different from, but complementary to, the classifications that a Scripture scholar might use.

Much of how you choose to proclaim a text will depend on its style, so it's important that you can distinguish among these three styles. Almost every book of the Bible contains examples of all three styles, so you can't always identify the style by the source of the text alone. But I will point out in which books certain styles predominate.

Narrative (Story) Text

This is the most straightforward style of text. A narrative text tells a story. Scripture is full of good stories. Even people who've never opened a Bible are familiar with some Bible stories. In these stories there are characters, places, and action, much like a children's bedtime story. The point of view is that of the narrator, but often there is dialogue from one, two, or more characters. Whenever you have a text that's concerned with who, what, when, and where, you have a narrative text. Examples include the creation story (Genesis), the Passover story (Exodus), and the story of the early Church (Acts). Much of what we proclaim from the Pentateuch or history books is narrative, as are some parts of the prophetic books. In the New Testament, the synoptic Gospels are mostly narrative. There is also some narrative in the letters.

Here's one example of a narrative text (2 Kings 4:42–44; Ordinary 17B[1]):

 It's very important for actors to know the style of play they are working with. Beyond the simple division of comedy or drama, there are styles such as Elizabethan verse, Restoration comedy, satire, farce, theater of the absurd, comedy of manners, and so on. Styles exist in film and television too. Sitcoms are played in a certain style; detective shows, one-hour dramas, telenovelas—all different styles, each requiring a different style of acting. It would be very strange if everyone on a crime drama started playing the lines as though it were a sitcom! The style tells actors a great deal about how they must interpret the text.

> A man came from Baal-shalishah bringing
>> to Elisha, the man of God,
>>> twenty barley loaves made from the firstfruits,
>>>> and fresh grain in the ear.
> Elisha said, "Give it to the people to eat."
> But his servant objected,
>> "How can I set this before a hundred people?"
> Elisha insisted, "Give it to the people to eat.

---

1. Proper 12B. (For an explanation of this citation style, please see page 6.)

For thus says the LORD,

    'They shall eat and there shall be some left over.'"

    And when they had eaten, there was some left over,

    as the LORD had said

 Sometimes, a narrative text occurs within another text—a story within a story. This is especially the case with Gospel excerpts that include parables. We start with one story—the story of Jesus' ministry—and then switch to the story of the parable that Jesus tells, and then sometimes return to continue the first narrative of Jesus' ministry. These parables should be treated as a narrative text separate from the narrative of Jesus' ministry.

Didactic (Teaching) Text

The purpose of didactic text is to teach or explain a point. Didactic texts are frequently taken from the epistles but also from the history books, prophets, and wisdom books. The record of Jesus' teachings in the Gospels is usually didactic text. Here are two examples of didactic text:

Beloved:

Christ suffered for sins once,

    the righteous for the sake of the unrighteous,

    that he might lead you to God.

Put to death in the flesh,

    he was brought to life in the Spirit.

In it he also went to preach to the spirits in prison,

    who had once been disobedient

    while God patiently waited in the days of Noah

    during the building of the ark,

    in which a few persons, eight in all,

    were saved through water.

This prefigured baptism, which saves you now.

                          (1 Peter 3:18–21a; Lent 1B)

God did not make death,

    nor does he rejoice in the destruction of the living.

For he fashioned all things that they might have being;

    and the creatures of the world are wholesome,

    and there is not a destructive drug among them

    nor any domain of the netherworld on earth,

    for justice is undying.   (Wisdom 1:13–15; Ordinary 13B[2])

---

2. Proper 8B.

Exhortatory Text

An exhortatory text makes an urgent appeal to its listeners. It may encourage them, warn them, or challenge them. It often includes a call to action; it tells the listeners what to do. Sometimes, the exhortation is directed to God, pleading for mercy or justice or praising God's goodness and love. The speaker is sometimes the writer; sometimes God directly addresses the people. The two primary sources of exhortatory texts are the prophets and the epistles, but there is also exhortatory text in the Gospels, especially John. We often read exhortatory text on Sundays, for obvious reasons, and these texts are some of the most exciting to proclaim.

Be aware that exhortatory text often looks very similar to didactic text, but the tone is different. There is a sense of urgency to the teaching. It sounds like a rallying cry, a campaign speech, a coach's pep talk to the team when they're behind in the game. It often conveys good news, very good news, in fact ("Don't be afraid! God is good! Rejoice!"), but it can also convey a warning ("Straighten up! God is angry! Stop acting stupid!").

Here are some clues to help you identify exhortatory text:

❧ Strong, heightened language, often punctuated with exclamation points in the translation

> Rise up in splendor, Jerusalem! Your light has come,
>> the glory of the Lord shines upon you. (Isaiah 60:1)

> Woe to the complacent in Zion! (Amos 6:1a)

> You brood of vipers! (Matthew 3:7b)

❧ Direct address to the people or to God

> Have you forgotten that encouraging text
>> in which you are addressed as sons? (Hebrews 12:5a, NJB)

> All you who are thirsty,
>> come to the water! (Isaiah 55:1a)

> How long, O Lord? I cry for help
>> but you do not listen! (Habakkuk 1:2a)

> "O Lord of hosts, you who test the just." (Jeremiah 20:12a)

❧ Commands and calls to action

> Seek the Lord while he may be found,
>> call him while he is near. (Isaiah 55:6)

> I charge you to do all that you have been told, with no faults or failures,
>> until the appearing of our Lord Jesus Christ.
>>> (1 Timothy 6:13c–14, NJB)

> Fear no one. (Matthew 10:26a)

Beyond Reading: Advanced Training for Proclaimers of the Word of God

✤ Key words and phrases such as *listen, hear, truly I say*

Now, Israel, hear the statutes and decrees

which I am teaching you to observe.   (Deuteronomy 4:1a)

Hear, O Israel, the commandments of life:

listen, and know prudence!   (Baruch 3:9)

Although most readings are primarily in one of these three styles, some may be in a mix of styles. The following passage, for example, starts as a narrative and then quotes an exhortatory teaching:

The Spirit drove Jesus out into the desert,

and he remained in the desert for forty days, tempted by Satan.

He was among wild beasts,

and the angels ministered to him.

After John had been arrested,

Jesus came to Galilee proclaiming the gospel of God:

"This is the time of fulfillment.

The kingdom of God is at hand.

Repent, and believe in the gospel."   (Mark 1:12–15; Lent 1B)

Identify Literary Devices

After identifying the overall style, go through the text and identify any *literary devices* that the author employs. These devices can reveal an enormous amount about the meaning of the passage. It's critical that you understand them so you can use them to convey this meaning in your proclamation.

Poetry is often used in exhortatory texts, as it is a great way to heighten language. But poetry is sometimes used in narrative texts and didactic texts as well, simply because poetic text is easier to remember than prose text. Poetry was used as a mnemonic device for some stories and teachings. In fact, whenever you see poetry in the Bible, know that the text was written not to be read but to be sung (or at least chanted). Try reciting the words to the national anthem; then try singing it. You can see for yourself that it's much easier to remember words set to music.

There are a few problems with identifying poetry in our texts, however. First of all, Hebrew poetry doesn't rhyme, and though it often has a specific rhythm, that rhythm may be lost in the translation. Second, poetry is especially difficult to translate because both the meaning and the poetic sense must be translated. Thus, translators sometimes turn what was poetry in the original text into prose in the translation. Translators also disagree on what should actually be considered poetry. In some translations (the New Jerusalem, for example), much of the Gospel of John is considered and printed as poetry. In other translations (NRSV, for one), little of it is. Third, poetry doesn't always look like poetry in a printed translation; that is, it's sometimes printed in paragraph form rather than in verse form. In lectionaries, the opposite is sometimes true, and all texts look like poetry because all readings are printed with short lines called *sense lines* to aid proclamation.

Ultimately, it may be of little importance to establish whether your reading contains poetry or not. The other literary devices used in the reading will be more helpful to your proclamation than knowing whether you are reading poetry or prose. Still, if you know that you have a poetic text, you should consider why the author chose to put the text into the form of a poem. Was it to make the text exhortatory, or was it so people would remember the teaching?

Parallelism refers to phrases or sentences that have a similar structure or express a similar idea, as in these examples:

> He has clothed me with a robe of salvation,
> and wrapped me in a mantle of justice. (Isaiah 61:10b)

> I will bless those who bless you
> and curse those who curse you. (Genesis 12:3a)

> Remain in me, as I remain in you. (John 15:4a)

 Parallelism is one of the most frequently used literary devices in both the Old and New Testaments. Many of the sayings of Jesus display parallelism, including the Beatitudes (Matthew 5:1–12; Luke 6:20–26) and the Golden Rule (Matthew 7:12; Luke 6:31). The following is a strong four-line example:

> Do not judge, and you will not be judged;
> do not condemn, and you will not be condemned.
> Forgive, and you will be forgiven; give, and it will be given to you.
>
> (Luke 6:37–38a, NRSV)

Sections of a reading can also parallel each other, as in the following passage from Jeremiah. This passage also uses *simile*, in which one thing is compared to another using the words *like* or *as*. In the first part of this reading, the author says those who rely on human strength are like a shrub that has to struggle for survival. In the parallel second part, the author says those who rely on God are like a tree that flourishes despite harsh conditions.

> Thus says the LORD:
> Cursed are those who trust in mere mortals
> and make mere flesh their strength,
> whose hearts turn away from the LORD.
> They shall be like a shrub in the desert,
> and shall not see when relief comes.
> They shall live in the parched places of the wilderness,
> in an uninhabited salt land.

Blessed are those who trust in the LORD,
>   whose trust is the LORD.
They shall be like a tree planted by water,
>   sending out its roots by the stream.
It shall not fear when heat comes,
>   and its leaves shall stay green;
in the year of drought it is not anxious,
>   and it does not cease to bear fruit.

(Jeremiah 17:5–8, NRSV, Ordinary 6C[3])

Paul uses a great deal of parallelism in his letters, as it is an excellent teaching device. Look at how Paul explains to the Corinthians that the idea that we will have a body at the resurrection proceeds from our having a body while we are on earth. He draws parallels between Adam and Christ, between earthliness and heavenliness:

Brothers and sisters:

It is written, *The first man, Adam, became a living being,*
>   the last Adam a life-giving spirit.
But the spiritual was not first;
>   rather the natural and then the spiritual.

The first man was from the earth, earthly;
>   the second man, from heaven.
As was the earthly one, so also are the earthly,
>   and as is the heavenly one, so also are the heavenly.
Just as we have borne the image of the earthly one,
>   we shall also bear the image of the heavenly one.

(1 Corinthians 15:45–49; Ordinary Time 7C[4])

Identifying these instances of parallel construction is essential to understanding your text. Once you find them, you will use parallelism to help your listeners understand the reading as well.

There are also two more subtle types of parallelism you need to look for. The first is *thought rhyme*, and it is a hallmark of Hebrew poetry. Hebrew poets showed their skill not in the cleverness of their rhymes but in their ability to be deeply descriptive of a thing or idea. Consider this passage from Sirach:

For great is the wisdom of the Lord;
>   he is mighty in power and sees everything;

his eyes are on those who fear him,
>   and he knows every human action.

---

3. Epiphany 6C.
4. Epiphany 7C.

He has not commanded anyone to be wicked,
>> and he has not given anyone permission to sin.

(Sirach 15:18–20 NRSV; Ordinary 6A[5])

I've separated out the couplets so you can see more clearly that both lines of each couplet say basically the same thing, but each line says it in a different way. In thought rhyme, sometimes the second line expands on the thought in the first, sometimes it makes it more specific, sometimes it even contrasts the idea. Thought rhyme occurs throughout wisdom literature and the prophets.

The second subtle type of parallelism, *paradox*, uses parallel construction to express an idea that seems to contradict itself. Jesus often employs paradox to show that life in the reign of God will turn our expectations upside down:

For whoever wishes to save his life will lose it,
>> but whoever loses his life for my sake will save it.   (Luke 9:24)

Thus, the last will be first, and the first will be last.   (Matthew 20:16a)

For everyone who exalts himself will be humbled,
>> but the one who humbles himself will be exalted.   (Luke 14:11)

 Whenever a strong parallelism breaks down, take note! There is something significant the author wants to stress, as in this passage:

This saying is trustworthy:
If we have died with him
>> we shall also live with him;
if we persevere
>> we shall also reign with him.
But if we deny him
>> he will deny us.
If we are unfaithful
>> he remains faithful,
>> for he cannot deny himself.   (2 Timothy 2:11–13; Ordinary 28C[6])

Based on the parallelism Paul establishes, we would expect the last line to read: "If we are unfaithful he will be unfaithful." The break with parallelism thus shows that the author is making a very significant point.

Repetition of the same word or phrase over the course of a reading is another device an author uses to emphasize a point. A direct repetition of a single word (*I, I; Amen, Amen*) is a device used to stress what follows. Make sure it doesn't sound like you're repeating yourself. Each instance should sound different. Heighten the second instance of the word:

---

5. Epiphany 6A.
6. Proper 23C.

I, I am He

> who blots out your transgressions for my own sake,
>
> > and I will not remember your sins.　　　　　(Isaiah 43:25 NRSV)

Rejoice with Jerusalem . . . ;

> exult, exult with her,
>
> > all you who were mourning over her!　　　　　(Isaiah 66:10)

In the following passage from Matthew, the idea of fear and fearlessness is repeated four times. Again, when you proclaim, make each instance distinct; build the intensity of the commands to "do not be afraid."

> Jesus said to the Twelve:
>
> "*Fear no one.*
>
> Nothing is concealed that will not be revealed,
>
> > nor secret that will not be known.
>
> What I say to you in the darkness, speak in the light;
>
> > what you hear whispered, proclaim on the housetops.
>
> And *do not be afraid* of those who kill the body but cannot kill the soul;
>
> > rather, *be afraid* of the one who can destroy
> >
> > both soul and body in Gehenna.
>
> Are not two sparrows sold for a small coin?
>
> Yet not one of them falls to the ground
>
> > without your Father's knowledge.
> >
> > Even all the hairs of your head are counted.
>
> So *do not be afraid*; you are worth more than many sparrows."
>
> > > (Matthew 10:26–31; Ordinary 12A[7]; emphasis mine)

Often, we breeze through a reading without stopping to notice literary devices. But we must pay attention because these devices tell us a lot about the meaning of the text that we must convey. Mark the instances of these devices on the rehearsal copy of your reading; you will use all these devices in your work.

Read the Contexts

Actors joke that a self-involved actor sees the script as "*Blah blah blah*. My line! *Blah blah blah*. My line!" Although actors obviously focus their rehearsal work on the scenes they are part of, they must also be aware of what comes before and after their scenes as well as what happens in scenes they aren't in. In order to be informed enough to play a specific role, an actor needs to know the entire story of the play, even if the actor's specific character disappears midway through.

7.　Proper 7A.

Identifying Choice Words

Have you ever seen a copy of the first printing of Shakespeare's plays? Aside from some funny looking letter *f*'s (which are actually the letter *s*), some words are in italics, and some words that are not proper nouns are capitalized. Many editors have long assumed that these were just printing errors or "the way things were printed" back then. But some have a different theory. Some scholars believe that these words were intended to be set apart by Shakespeare. Why? Because he wanted the actor to take note of them especially.

Elizabethan actors did not have weeks of rehearsal to put together a play. They couldn't afford to have the theater closed for that long. Sometimes a play would be rehearsed in an afternoon and first performed that evening. Since there was little time to memorize lines, actors carried a copy of their lines onto stage with them. (Their part was printed on a roll of paper like a scroll so they could unroll it as the play progressed. That's why we call the part an actor plays a *role*. Some classical paintings of actors show them holding such a roll.) The actors couldn't be expected to be very familiar with the text, so Shakespeare highlighted certain words as a cue to the actor to make a strong choice about how they played those words.

Choice words in Scripture (sometimes called operative words) are the significant words that a proclaimer should notice. Choice words shouldn't necessarily be stressed (more about that in the next chapter), but they should be noted. They are the key words that an effective proclaimer uses to convey the meaning, emotion, and intent of the reading.

We've all heard lectors who read each word as though it were as insignificant as the next, and we've all heard lectors who read . . . each . . . word . . . as . . . though . . . it . . . were . . . the . . . most . . . important . . . in . . . the . . . text. But some words *are* more important than others. There are at least two or three choice words per verse, sometimes more.

Here are some guidelines for identifying choice words:

✤ Words that are parallel or paradoxical are always choice words.

> Is not man's *life* on earth a *drudgery*?
>> Are not his *days* those of *hirelings*?
>> He is a *slave* who longs for the *shade*,
>> a *hireling* who waits for his *wages*. (Job 7:1)

> The *last* will be *first*, and the *first* will
>> be *last*.   (Matthew 20:16a)

✤ Words with a strong emotional content such as *love*, *hate*, *death*, *famine*, *hunger*, and *thirst* are often choice words.

> In those days, in their *thirst* for water,
>> the people grumbled against Moses.
>>>   (Exodus 17:3)

> No one can serve two masters.
> He will . . . *hate* one and *love* the other.
>>   (Matthew 6:24)

✤ Exclusive modifiers—such as *always*, *never*, *all*, *everything*, and *nothing*—along with comparative modifiers—such as *greater*, *greatest*, *less*, and *least*—are good choice words.

> He is before *all* things,
>> and in him *all* things hold together.
>>>   (Colossians 1:17)

> The foolishness of God is *wiser* than
>> human wisdom.   (1 Corinthians 1:25)

✤ Verbs, especially action verbs and command verbs (*hear*, *do*, *do not*, and so forth), can be choice words, especially if no other choice words seem to be present.

> You who are Israelites, *hear* these words.
>>   (Acts 2:22)

> *See*, I am doing something new!
>>   (Isaiah 43:19)

Here is a verse with choice words highlighted:

Oh, *come* to the water *all* you who
are *thirsty*;
though you have no money, *come!*
Buy and *eat*; *come*, buy wine and milk
without money, *free!*   (Isaiah 55:1 NJB)

Note again that these words are not necessarily stressed in a proclamation, but some choice must be made about them. Choice words can be helpful in discerning the meaning of a troublesome text. Paying close attention to verbs, in particular, can give you a feel for the text that you might otherwise miss. We'll talk more about what to do with choice words in the next few chapters.

In the same way, you should be aware of the *context* in which your reading occurs. There are actually three contexts to familiarize yourself with:

1. The first is the *scriptural context*—that is, the verses before and after the excerpt in Scripture.

2. The second is the *liturgical context*—that is, the other readings that are proclaimed that day and the character of the season.

3. The third is the *lectionary context*—that is, the readings proclaimed the previous week and those to be proclaimed the following week.

Just as actors would spend little time on the scenes they aren't in, it's not necessary to spend a great deal of time on context. But you need to be at least familiar with all three of these contexts as you prepare.

The scriptural context is important because a lectionary is not Scripture but rather a *collection of excerpts* (called *pericopes*—per-IK-uh-peez) from Scripture. Reading the chapters before and after each excerpt, especially before, is most helpful. The assembly will not know this context, unless it was recently read, but your knowledge of it will help you understand much better what you proclaim.

The liturgical and lectionary contexts are both found in the lectionary. Reading the other readings of the day and the readings of the previous and following weeks will help you understand why these particular excerpts were chosen and therefore what particular meaning is to be stressed in the reading.

To read the liturgical and lectionary contexts fruitfully, you should understand how the lectionary is organized:

The first reading is usually from the Old Testament, the second reading is from one of the New Testament letters, and the third reading is always from one of the four Gospels. (The psalm between the first two readings is yet another reading, and you should be familiar with it as well. Be aware, though, that discretion is allowed in choosing a psalm, so the one in the lectionary may not be the one used in your community. The verse before the Gospel is also usually taken from Scripture, but as with the psalm, a different verse might be used in the celebration.)

The Gospels rotate on a three-year cycle. In year A the Gospels come from Matthew, in year B they come from Mark, and in year C from Luke. We hear John during the Easter season in all three years and also in the middle of year B, because Mark is a short Gospel.

The readings are chosen to be either *continuous or complementary*.

Outside major seasons (during Ordinary Time), the second reading and the Gospel are *continuous*; that is, they pick up very close to where they left off the previous week. Sometimes there is a bit of a gap between weeks, sometimes no gap at all. The first reading is not continuous from week to week but rather is chosen to *complement* the Gospel in some way. Sometimes the relationship between the two is obvious. For example, when the Gospel story of Jesus' healing of the leper is read (Mark 1:40–45; Ordinary 6B[8]), the first reading relates the Mosaic law about leprosy (Leviticus 13:1–2, 44–46) to remind us that lepers were outcasts of society. Sometimes the relationship is less obvious, however, and a particular theme in the Gospel may only be echoed quietly in the first reading.

Ordinary time

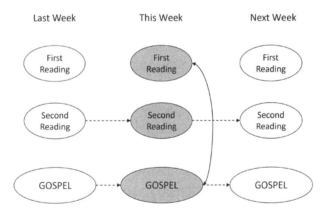

 This arrangement of first readings applies to the Roman Catholic, Episcopal, and Lutheran lectionaries and is given as an option in the *Revised Common Lectionary* (RCL), used in many other churches. The RCL also provides a series of first readings that are *continuous* and thus not specifically related to the Gospel. If your community uses the RCL, be sure you know which option is being used.

During Advent, Christmas Time, and Lent, and on solemnities, feasts, and memorials, all three readings are chosen to be *complementary*. That is, all three readings are reflections on the particular aspects of the Christian mystery being celebrated at that time. During the Easter season, the first reading is a continuous reading from the Acts of the Apostles exploring the life and growth of the early Church, and the second reading is a continuous reading of either 1 Peter (year A), 1 John (year B), or Revelation (year C). Thus, during Christmas, Lent, and Advent, all three readings relate more closely to the liturgical context than they do to the lectionary context.

---

8. Epiphany 6B.

Christmas, Lent, Advent, and Feasts

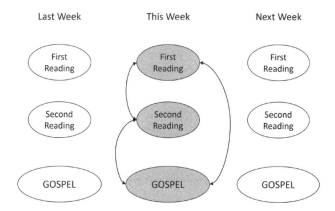

Easter season

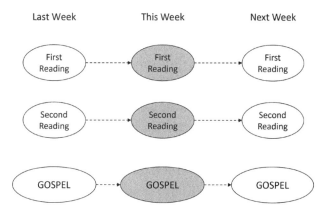

 If your reading is *continuous*, it will be most helpful to focus on the prior week's corresponding reading. If your reading is *complementary*, it will be most helpful to focus on the other readings of the day that complement it. That said, you should always read all three contexts. In fact, for practical reasons, you should be sure to read the other readings of the day in case you are called on to proclaim them if the assigned lector doesn't show up.

Study the Commentaries

While you're reading the scriptural context, you'll also want to read what the commentaries say about your passage. See what comments are given about the point the writer was trying to make. Learn about the circumstances of the writer and the intended audience. What was going on in the history of the biblical world at the time the reading was composed? Make sure you also understand the cultural context of the reading. These texts were written in and for a society very different from ours in time, place, and custom. For example, there are many texts in both the Old and New Testaments about people dining together. What significance did a shared meal have in Semitic culture?

Don't get so wrapped up in Scripture study that you neglect the practice of your proclamation skills, however. Coming to an understanding of the reading is essential, but then you need to work with your voice so that what you've learned can be heard in your proclamation. Remember, you are a proclaimer! So don't spend all your time in the library instead of on the practice field.

Read the Passage in Another Translation

There are two dominant categories of Bible translation. The first is *literal translation*, which strives for what is called *formal equivalence*—as close to a word-for-word translation as possible. The second category is *sense translation*, which strives for *dynamic equivalence*—a thought-for-thought translation—trying to express in English the *sense or meaning* of what was said in the original language, without being slavish to a word-for-word construction. For example, a sense translation of the French greeting, *Comment allez-vous?* would be "How are you doing?" A literal translation would be "How go you?" A third category, looser and less common, is *paraphrase*, which simply paraphrases the passage from the original language.

In practice, Bible translations fall somewhere on a continuum between literal and sense. Those that lean more toward the literal, formal side include the Revised Standard Version (RSV), the New Revised Standard Version (NRSV), the New American Bible Revised Edition (NABRE), the New American Bible (NAB), and the New King James Bible (NKJV). The Revised New Jerusalem Bible (RNJB) is considered somewhat less literal than these, as is the New International Version (NIV), yet both are more literal than those recognized as sense translations. The New Jerusalem Bible (NJB), though more literal than its predecessor, the Jerusalem Bible, leans into the sense category; the Contemporary English Version (CEV), and the Good News Translation (GNT), formerly called Today's English Version (TEV), are definitely sense translations that use informal, colloquial English—and so are considered especially appropriate for young people.

Bible translations chosen as the basis for lectionaries in Christian communities have struck some balance between the literal, word-for-word and the sense, thought-for-thought approach to translation. Although lectionaries are said to be "based on" a particular translation, they make many adaptations, so there are differences between the form of the reading in the lectionary and its Bible counterpart. The New American Bible Revised Edition (NABRE) serves as the basis for the Roman Catholic *Lectionary for Mass* in the United States; the New Revised Standard Version (NRSV) is the basis for Roman Catholic Lectionary for English-speaking Canada and for the Revised Common Lectionary used by many Protestant communities. The Jerusalem Bible of 1966 is the basis for Roman Catholic lectionaries of Australia, England and Wales, Scotland, Ireland, India, New Zealand, Pakistan, and South Africa. (It is as yet unclear whether any of those lectionaries might be revised now that the Revised New Jerusalem translation has been published.) The Contemporary English Version (CEV) presently serves as the basis for the *Catholic Lectionary for Masses with Children* in the United States.

Sometimes it can be helpful to see how a difficult passage is rendered in a different translation, especially if you compare a more literal translation with one closer to a sense translation. But even comparing within the same categories (literal or sense) can bring new insights. And, of course, a different translation may have different explanatory notes. Many of the translations cited above are available online. Be cautious, however, about using other translations you find online. Stick to those that are known to rest on solid, recent biblical scholarship.

Read the Text Out Loud

This would seem to be obvious, but you'd be amazed at how many lectors I encounter who prepare with their texts only by reading them silently. As I noted previously, proclamation is not primarily an intellectual activity; it is a physical activity. You *must* get the words into your mouth so you can know what they feel like. Stand up when you practice as well. Not only will you be more accurately reproducing the circumstances of your proclamation, but you'll get new insights into the reading when you speak it out loud. (You won't be able to be silent to use the techniques in this book, anyway!)

Speak the Text Casually

This is a very powerful and helpful technique. Read the text as if it were a conversation with a friend over coffee. Literal translations are not written in a very conversational style, and even sense translations may use "formal" language. This can make it more difficult to discern meaning. Reading the text casually can help in this. Read a narrative text as if you were telling the story to your friend. Read a didactic or exhortatory text as if you were trying to convince your friend of the point of the reading.

This technique will make you more comfortable in seeing the text as something to work with and, more important, to play with. It takes a willingness to play with these texts to create an effective proclamation. Speaking the text casually helps change any perception that these texts are fossils meant to be enshrined in a museum. They are living, breathing words, and they can withstand some rough treatment in practice. In fact, the text will reveal all sorts of things to you when you practice it this way.

Make note of the following impressions, or of any others that occur to you:

❀ What is the author's intent? What is the author saying?

❀ What is the author's feeling? What do *you* feel as you speak the text this way?

❀ What words do you naturally stress? Do you find a rhythm?

I recommend using this technique frequently. When I'm working with lectors in a church, I'll ask them to come down from the ambo (the lectern in the worship space from which the Scriptures are proclaimed) and stand in the pews or even sit next to me and read the text. This takes them out of their official "lector mode" and helps them personalize and demystify the text. Their transformation from reader into storyteller is usually quite profound. They then take the discoveries made in storytelling back to the ambo for their proclamation, which is inevitably more nuanced and engaging.

The exercise is also useful for getting an idea of what the original author of the text was feeling as the story was being composed. Actors are challenged to make their lines seem like real conversation. We usually don't rehearse what we're going to say before we say it; the words spill out from our need to communicate. Yet actors, like lectors, already know what they are going to say. They must find a way to make these words sound fresh, as though they were being spoken for the first time. A casual read can help with this.

Both actors and lectors also suffer from knowing the end of the story. This knowledge naturally informs our reading of the text. But this can also lead us into the trap of *playing the end at the beginning*. This is called *telegraphing*, and it robs our proclamation of its immediacy.

As you prepare, pay attention to those parts of the text that would be surprising or scandalous or challenging if you didn't know the end. For example, when Jesus says that he is going to Jerusalem to be put to death (Matthew 16:21; Mark 8:31; Luke 9:22), this isn't surprising news to us. But it was shocking news to his disciples. If you were telling this to one of your friends who didn't know the story, you wouldn't blithely gloss over such a declaration. In the same way, give it the weight it deserves in your proclamation.

Write the Text

An old actor's trick for memorizing lines is to write out the text, preferably by hand. Even though your goal is not memorization (more on that later), it can be very helpful to use this technique. There's something about writing that forces you to connect with and own the text in a way that reading and rereading just do not accomplish.

Paraphrase the Text

When I'm directing a play and actors are having trouble with a scene, I will ask them to drop their scripts and improvise the scene. The goal is not to create a new scene, but to play basically the same scene without being constrained by the lines as written. You don't really know what a text means until you are able to put it in your own words. I challenge you not to finish your work on a text until you are comfortable paraphrasing it.

Paraphrase without looking at the text; then check your work against the text, taking note of the parts that you left out of your paraphrase. You'll discover

Beyond Reading: Advanced Training for Proclaimers of the Word of God

that you remember the parts that are most vibrant and meaningful to you, so you'll want to find ways to make the other parts just as vibrant and meaningful. (For help on this, see the exercises on imagination in chapter 6.)

Paraphrasing can also give you some of the same insights as speaking casually. When you're freed from reading exact lines, you may notice new feelings or intentions. You may discover new and deeper meanings. And you may feel where energy and emphasis shift in the text. Use all these insights when you return to the text. When actors are finished improvising, I immediately ask them to start the scene as written so the intentions and emotions they discovered in the improvisation are carried over into the scene. You may wish to do the same. (You can also write the text in paraphrase, but speaking it may lead to more discoveries.)

Walk the Text

Another interesting exercise is to walk the text. Read the text aloud, walking as you do so, and every time a new thought occurs in the text, change your direction. (You can also change direction at every punctuation mark or every time a new character speaks.) Linking physical activity to a text can be very helpful. Sometimes, in rehearsal for a play, I'll forget my line but remember my movement; once I execute the movement, the line returns.

This exercise will also help you see how the text itself "changes direction." You may find that you're walking mostly in one direction for the entire text, so you know you have a pretty cohesive reading. Or you may have to fly all over the room, changing directions many times, so you'll see that you have a more complex text with multiple thoughts or characters.

Identify Pronunciation Challenges

As you read over the text, be certain to note words you're not sure how to pronounce. A good dictionary or pronunciation guide is essential.

Don't assume that you only need to look up proper names. You may want to double-check the pronunciation of common words you think you know. I once had an entire room full of actors turn on me when I pronounced the word theater as thee-AY-ter. (It's THEE-uh-ter.) I never mispronounced it again!

Use standard American pronunciation (or the standard pronunciation of the language and dialect of your community), even if you know the Hebrew or Greek pronunciations. To communicate these stories so people understand them, you need to use standard pronunciations that are familiar to them.

Pray the Text

While prayer should precede and suffuse all your work as a lector, praying with the text itself is a critical part of your preparation. There are many different ways to pray with Scripture text. You may already have a favorite way; if so, use it with your text. If not, you can simply read and meditate on your text during your regular prayer time. You can easily find suggestions for how to do this online. If you proclaim a narrative text, you may choose to imagine yourself in the story as one of the characters or as an onlooker. If you proclaim a didactic or exhortatory text, you may imagine yourself as the original proclaimer or writer of the text, or as one of the first hearers. (More on active imagination in chapter 6.) If your text speaks directly to God, you can use it *as your prayer*.

Whatever method you use, take note of four things:

1. What words, phrases, or images strike you as you read, pray, meditate, or imagine the text?

2. What feelings come up as you pray the text, especially around those images that strike you?

3. What do you think the Spirit is saying to you through this passage, or what new learning do you come away with?

4. What is your response to what the Spirit is saying?

If you choose, you can form your prayer around these questions. In your prayer time, read your passage once, slowly and carefully, and pay attention to words or images that strike you. You can stop and meditate on those images. Then read it again, paying attention to your feelings. Then read it a third time, listening for God's message for you. Then a fourth time, considering what your response will be. This is a variation on the ancient Christian prayer practice known as lectio divina. You could do this all in one session, or spread it out over four or more times.

This is one reason you shouldn't wait until the week before your proclamation to work with your reading. The Spirit may have all sorts of insights to give you as you pray, and you need time to work with them in your proclamation.

Memorization

Before we leave our discussion of text, I want to address the question of memorization. Some lectors prefer to memorize the text they proclaim, but I recommend against this, for a number of reasons.

First, recalling the text from memory adds another stressor to your proclamation. Having to focus even a small part of your energy on recalling the text means you have that much less to focus on good proclamation.

Second, a person reciting from memory is a distraction to the assembly. You may be proclaiming magnificently, but there will be people focusing only on the fact that you haven't looked down at the lectionary. Some may even be nervous for you that you'll miss a line. I can't tell you how many times I've walked offstage after a performance and met an audience member whose first comment was not "I loved your performance" or "Your emotional honesty was amazing" or even "That was the worst thing I've ever seen." No, the comment I've received most often is "How did you remember all those lines?" (I'm tempted to respond, "Well, I only had to remember them one at a time!") People are amazed at the ability to memorize, and if you show them you have this skill, they'll probably be more impressed with that skill than with the Word you proclaim.

Third, you need to show that your proclamation is grounded in the book. We are storytellers, yes, but of a specific story that has been handed down to us in a book. The assembly needs to know that you're not making up the story you proclaim but that it's the story as it is "in the book."

Now it's possible that you'll become so familiar with the text through your preparation that you'll memorize it unintentionally. *Bravo!* This means you've really done your work with the text, but I still recommend using the book. You'll have no problem making eye contact with the assembly if you're that comfortable with the text, but you should still look down at the lectionary every couple of lines or so, just to let the community know you're proclaiming the story from the book.

Final Thoughts on Text

Over the course of your work preparing for proclamation, you'll come back again and again to the text. Everything in our proclamation flows from this text, and everything we do returns to it for validation. I look at the single volume on my shelf that contains the collected works of Shakespeare. It's such a small and unassuming book really, when I think of the centuries of powerful performances that have sprung from the words it contains. The same is true, even more so, of the Scripture we cherish. We lectors are charged with the awesome task of wresting a mighty power from nothing more than a few cubic inches of paper and ink.

Seven Important Things to Remember about Text

1. Take your time with the first read-through. Record your initial impressions before you move on to more detailed work.

2. Identify the style of your text:
   - ✤ narrative (story) text
   - ✤ didactic (teaching) text
   - ✤ exhortatory text

3. Identify the literary devices used:
   - ✤ parallelism
   - ✤ thought rhyme
   - ✤ paradox
   - ✤ repetition
   - ✤ simile

4. Read the contexts:

    ❋ the scriptural context (verses before and after the excerpt)

    ❋ the liturgical context (the other readings of the day and the character of the season)

    ❋ the lectionary context (the readings from the previous and following weeks)

5. Do your scriptural research, using a study Bible, commentaries, websites, and other resources. Understand the time period, audience, and culture of the author.

6. Practice with the text by speaking it casually and by paraphrasing it.

7. Pray with the text. Ask the Spirit for wisdom as you discern what the text is saying to you.

Chapter 3

Working on Voice: Speak in a Loud, Clear Voice, and Try Not to Bump into the Ambo

A famous actor was once asked to divulge the key to his success. "I speak," he said, "in a loud, clear voice, and try not to bump into the furniture." Of course, it was a deliberate understatement, but the point is valid: the most basic asset of actors is their voice. (The quotation has been variously attributed to actors from Alfred Lunt to Spencer Tracy to Russell Crowe, so you know it has a kernel of truth.)

The same is true for a proclaimer. We work with *oral* stories, which were "written" in voices long before they were written in ink. Except for the epistles and a few books of the Old Testament, most of what we have inherited as Scripture started out as oral tradition and followed the path described earlier. The evangelists were not stenographers, taking dictation directly from Jesus and writing it down on the first-century equivalent of laptop computers. They, too, inherited a story from an oral tradition. Even the writings of Paul were dictated to a scribe. As storytellers, we take the written word and return it to the oral tradition from whence it came.

This is very important to remember: these stories belong to our tradition of storytelling as much as they belong to the Scripture scholar's tradition of exegesis. Our voices need to be trained and ready to put these stories where they belong—into the ears and hearts of the assembly. Half the life of the story belongs to the teller.

Don't be daunted by the technical nature of the work in this chapter. This work is akin to the drills that athletes run or the scales that musicians must practice. The legendary pianist Paderewski once said of this work, "If I miss one day of practice, I notice it. If I miss two days, the critics notice it. If I miss three days, the audience notices it." Just as in music, there are four basic elements to our work with voice: tempo, rhythm, volume, and pitch.

Tempo

Tempo refers to the speed of our proclamation—that is, how fast we talk. The most common mistake made by those new to public speaking is to go too fast. It's important for anyone who speaks publicly to watch their tempo, but it's even more important for lectors. Here's why:

First, the text you proclaim is difficult for a hearer to follow. Your listeners are most used to hearing normal, everyday speech. In fact, studies have shown that we "listen ahead" of what we hear; that is, we anticipate what will be said before it's actually said, based on our experience with conversational speech. However, most translations of Scripture are not written in conversational speech, especially the literal translations like those used as the basis for most lectionaries.

For this reason, it's harder for our brains to use the listen-ahead technique when we hear it proclaimed. Consequently, you need to slow down your proclamation so listeners can follow more easily. Remember, you have the advantage of having worked with the text for some time before your proclamation, but, for most of your community, it's the first time in a long time that they're hearing it.

Another reason for slowing down is that many churches have very poor acoustics for proclaiming. As a member of the community, you're probably already familiar with the acoustical challenges of your worship space. If not, or when you enter a new space, you should be cognizant of potential problems. If you are proclaiming in a space with poor acoustics, slowing down will help your listeners understand you.

Also keep in mind that when you are proclaiming at worship, your nerves and the rush of adrenaline from being "on" will likely cause you to read faster than you do in preparation. Thus, when rehearsing, focus on reading more slowly than you think you need to.

 A good rule of thumb is if you think you're going too slowly, you're probably going just right.

Trippingly on the Tongue

Walk backstage right before the curtain goes up on a play and you'll see the strangest rituals going on: actors in costume, bent over and shaking their heads and hands, massaging their faces, making weird and slightly rude noises with their lips, and someone in a corner talking very rapidly about Peter Piper or an overly industrious woodchuck. You may think that tongue twisters are nothing more than a source of fun for third-graders, but for actors they're . . . well, okay, they're actually a source of fun for actors, too.

These exercises also serve the useful purpose of loosening up your vocal apparatus. These twisters may seem like a waste of time, but an actor knows that the night they forget their warm-ups is the night they perform the Sinatra version of Hamlet's words: *Do be or not do be!*

General Warm-Ups

Red leather, yellow leather;
red leather, yellow leather.

Rubber baby buggy bumpers;
rubber baby buggy bumpers.

Toy boat; toy boat;
toy boat; toy boat.

Good blood, bad blood;
good blood, bad blood.

How much wood could a woodchuck chuck,
if a woodchuck could chuck wood?

She stood on the balcony, inexplicably
mimicking him hiccuping, and amicably
welcoming him in.

The sixth sick sheik's sixth sheep's sick.

This last is said to be the most difficult twister in the English language.

Working on B

Betty Botter bought some butter,
But it made her batter bitter.
So she bought some better butter;
Put it in the bitter batter.
Now the bitter batter's better.

A big black bug bit a big black bear
and the big black bear bled black blood.

For Working on Hard C and G

How many cuckoos could a good cook cook
if a good cook could cook cuckoos? As many
cuckoos as a good cook could cook if a good
cook could cook cuckoos.

For Working on M

Imagine an imaginary menagerie manager
imagining managing an imaginary menagerie.

For Working on P

Peter Piper picked a peck of pickled peppers.
If Peter Piper picked a peck of pickled peppers,
where's the peck of pickled peppers
Peter Piper picked?

For Working on R

Around the rock the rugged rascal ran;
the rugged rascal ran around the rock.

For Working on S

She sells seashells on the sea shore. On the sea
shore she sells seashells. The shells she sells
are seashells I am sure.

Sister Susie's sewing shirts for soldiers. Such
skill at sewing shirts my sweet young sister
Susie shows. Some soldiers send epistles, say
they'd sooner sleep in thistles, than the saucy
soft short shirts for soldiers Sister Susie sews.
A song from World War II.

For Working on T

A tutor who tooted the flute,
Tried to tutor two tooters to toot.
Said the two to the tutor,
"Is it harder to toot
Or to tutor two tooters to toot?"

For Working on *Th*

*For two thousand years, scholars have debated just who
Theophilus was, the person to whom Luke addressed his
Gospel (1:3) and the Acts of the Apostles (1:1). Finally, the
mystery is solved:*

Theophilus Thistle, the successful thistle sifter,
in sifting a sieve full of unsifted thistles, thrust
three thousand thistles through the thick of
his thumb.

Can you ever go too slowly? Absolutely. Lectors who read these sacred stories
too slowly often do so because they emphasize the *sacred* over the *story*. They
feel that by reading v-e-r-y s-l-o-w-l-y, they are showing their respect for the
holiness and seriousness of God's Word. But God's Word is meaningless if the
community doesn't understand it, and going too slowly will make it that much
more difficult to understand. Reading at a comprehensible pace is the best way
to respect the holiness of your proclamation.

How fast is too fast and how slow is too slow? The answer depends on many
factors, not only those we just discussed like acoustics, but also on individual
factors like timbre of voice and clarity of diction. (See the explanation of projection that follows and "Trippingly on the Tongue" on the previous page for
more on diction.)

For a rough check of your own pace, time yourself proclaiming the following reading. Try to read at the pace you usually use when proclaiming.

Then I, John, saw a new heaven and a new earth.
The former heaven and the former earth had passed away,
    and the sea was no more.

I also saw the holy city, a new Jerusalem,
    coming down out of heaven from God,
    prepared as a bride adorned for her husband.
I heard a loud voice from the throne saying,
    "Behold, God's dwelling is with the human race.
He will dwell with them and they will be his people
    and God himself will always be with them as their God.
    He will wipe every tear from their eyes,
    and there shall be no more death or mourning, wailing or pain,
    for the old order has passed away."

The One who sat on the throne said,
    "Behold, I make all things new."

(Revelation 21:1–5a; Easter 5C)

How did you do? If you finished the passage in less than forty-five seconds, you're probably reading too fast. Try reading it again and see if you can slow down. If you took more than seventy-five seconds to proclaim the passage, then you're probably going too slowly. Read it again and try to speed up, pause less, or take shorter pauses.

Rhythm

Rhythm is the beat of our speech. Rhythm refers to which words or syllables we stress and which we leave unstressed. A different rhythm can change the entire meaning of a sentence. For example, "Where were *you* last night?" is a different question from "Where were you *last* night?"

Finding the right rhythm can also reveal much about the *content* and *meaning* of the text. This is especially true in texts written specifically for proclamation or texts that come from an oral tradition like ours. The problem is that we work with translations of those stories, and sometimes, good rhythm had to be sacrificed for a better translation. Moreover, the rhythm present in the original language may be difficult or impossible to duplicate in the translation, Still, conscientious translators will pay attention to rhythm as they translate.

Here is a passage where rhythm is very pronounced. Read it aloud and see if you can find it:

Every writer has a rhythm; with some, the rhythm is very pronounced. Shakespeare and other writers in verse are the most obvious examples. But many prose writers—Neil Simon, David Mamet, and Harold Pinter come to mind immediately—have a particular rhythm, and actors ignore that rhythm at their peril. In comedy especially, finding the correct rhythm is usually the difference between a line getting a laugh and falling flat. There is an old saying that "Comedy is tragedy—with timing," and timing is all about rhythm.

> Strengthen the hands that are feeble,
>> make firm the knees that are weak,
>> say to those whose hearts are frightened:
>>> Be strong, fear not! (Isaiah 35:3–4a; Advent 3A)

Did you find it? If not, try it again, this time stressing the underlined syllables. Exaggerate the stresses as you speak so you can hear the rhythm.

> <u>Streng</u>then the <u>hands</u> that are <u>fee</u>ble,
>> make <u>firm</u> the <u>knees</u> that are <u>weak</u>,
>> say to <u>those</u> whose <u>hearts</u> are <u>frigh</u>tened:
>>> Be <u>strong</u>, fear <u>not</u>!

What do we learn about this reading when we find the rhythm? First, the rhythm helps us see that the first three lines show a strong parallelism. We'll want to make sure we bring that out in our proclamation. Finding the rhythm also forces us to add pauses around "Be strong" and "Fear not." This sets those phrases apart and gives them gravity.

Rhythm is one of the ways we bring out parallelism and paradox in a text.

> He has <u>clothed</u> me with a <u>robe</u> of sal<u>va</u>tion,
>> and <u>wrapped</u> me in a <u>man</u>tle of <u>jus</u>tice. (Isaiah 61:10b)

> I will <u>bless</u> those who <u>bless</u> you
>> and <u>curse</u> those who <u>curse</u> you. (Genesis 12:3a)

> For whoever wishes to <u>save</u> his life will <u>lose</u> it,
>> but whoever <u>loses</u> his life for <u>my</u> sake will <u>save</u> it. (Luke 9:24)

> Thus, the <u>last</u> will be <u>first</u>, and the <u>first</u> will be <u>last</u>. (Matthew 20:16a)

Incorrect stresses can obscure the parallel construction.

> <u>I</u> will bless those who <u>bless</u> you
>> and <u>curse</u> those who curse <u>you</u>.
> Thus, the last <u>will</u> be first, and the first <u>will</u> be last.

Entire readings also have rhythm. Rhythm shows us how a reading flows. It may have a long lyrical line from start to finish, or a series of short, terse statements, or a mix of the two. (The "walk the text" exercise is good for finding rhythm.) You'll find that shorter statements, like short words, call for a more staccato rhythm, while longer statements will do better proclaimed in a single, fluid line.

You can see that rhythm is a powerful tool not only for proclamation but also for understanding meaning. Whenever I am having problems with a particular passage in Shakespeare, I usually find that if I go back to the rhythm, the answers are there. Since we're dealing with translations, this isn't going to be as reliable a method for Scripture, but it's a very good place to look.

Pauses

As we just noted, pauses are an essential element to rhythm. I once wrote some music for the flute (which I don't play) that included long passages without any pauses, called *rests* in music. A friend of mine who was a flutist pointed out that the music was unplayable, as it didn't allow the musician a pause to take a breath! Pauses serve a similar function in speaking. They help establish rhythm, they establish where thoughts start and end, and they allow the proclaimer to take a breath.

Pausing in the right places is critical for effective proclamation. Pausing incorrectly or not at all can distort meaning. I remember one of my grammar school textbooks pointed out that "Let's eat, Grandma!" has a very different meaning from "Let's eat Grandma!"

The first and best source of information about where to pause is the punctuation used by the writer (or at least the translator). For purposes of speech, we divide punctuation into two classes:

1. Periods, question marks, and exclamation points are called "full-stops" because we typically come to a full stop in our speech and take a breath before beginning again.

2. Commas, semicolons, colons, and dashes are called "stops" because we usually take a break in our speech but rarely come to a full stop. We may or may not take a catch-up breath when we come to a stop.

 Semicolons and colons can also be used as full-stops, as they often are in the Roman Catholic *Lectionary for Mass* in the United States.

Of course, not all stops or full-stops carry the same weight. You may need to pause longer at some commas than at others in order to keep thoughts connected that need to be connected, and to separate thoughts that should be separated. Look at this example:

> All bitterness, fury, anger, shouting, and reviling
>
> must be removed from you, along with all malice.   (Ephesians 4:31)

You would pause briefly at the commas in the first line, which divide up a list of items that form one thought, and a bit longer at the comma in the second line, which sets off a secondary thought. You can take a quick catch-up breath if needed at the second-line comma and a full breath at the end of the line.

Some lectionaries are printed with *sense-line divisions*. This means that the lectionary designers have divided one sentence into two, three, or more printed lines. (See the previous example; the line is broken after "reviling.") Since sentences don't usually fit on one line of printed text, the sentences are broken at a place that keeps the sense clear, instead of just allowing the sentence to break wherever the margin happens to be. When possible, a sentence is broken at punctuation; but when it isn't, you must decide whether there should be a pause at the end of the printed line.

You don't need to pause at the end of every sense line! If two lines form one continuous thought (as in the above example), there should be no break between them.

Some lectionaries also insert a blank line between major sections of a reading. This spaces out the text into something resembling paragraphs or stanzas. It is often a good idea to pause at these places, as they usually indicate a significant shift in thought or story. In fact, this might be a place for a rather long pause, depending on how significant the shift is. Significant shifts may occur in a narrative text when a setting is changed, when there's a big jump in time, or when a new character is introduced. Significant shifts may occur in didactic or exhortatory texts when one line of reasoning or argument is concluded and another one begins.

All these are good visual cues for where to pause, but you will also need to add pauses in places where there is no punctuation or sense-line cue. Watch for the words *and, but, or, nor, so, since, because, then, which, that*, and so on. A pause is often (but not always) helpful before these words, especially when they introduce a secondary thought.

You will also want to pause to set off any significant thoughts or phrases in a reading. A longer pause may be helpful before such a thought, to prepare the community and give weight to what is said, as well as after the thought, to allow it to sink in before moving on. This is part of our natural speech pattern. We pause before and after we say something of significance, something we want to be sure our listener will really hear.

Meaning, above everything else, will be our guide in where to pause. Pauses should be used to keep thoughts together that go together and separate thoughts that don't. Longer pauses should be used to indicate significant shifts in thought or in the story.

Volume

Most lectors give very little thought to volume. They figure, I've got a microphone; as long as everyone can hear me, I needn't worry about volume. Yet volume is about more than just being heard. In fact, a better term to use is probably *vocal energy*. While volume refers to loudness or softness, vocal energy refers to where I direct my intention to speak and how strong that intention is.

When some people work with a mic, they drop their volume as well as their vocal energy and speak as though they were having an intimate conversation with someone just on the other side of the mic. The mic still picks up their voice, and they're still heard throughout the space, but their vocal energy drops off just past the ambo, and the community feels excluded from the proclamation. When people proclaim with good vocal energy, even though their volume might not be much higher, they speak as though they are communicating to the entire community. They direct their energy throughout the space by strengthening their intention to communicate with those farthest away. Think of it as the difference between speaking *into* the mic and speaking *through* the mic.

Vocal energy is strongly linked to eye contact, which I'll discuss in the next chapter.

Good vocal energy also allows more flexibility with volume. Volume should be varied in a reading to enhance meaning and story. It's only being faithful to the story to raise your volume when speaking commands ("Lazarus, come out!" "Shout for joy, O daughter Zion!") or accusations ("He has blasphemed!") or shouting ("Holy, holy, holy is the Lord of hosts!" "Crucify him!"). Just be sure to move back slightly from the microphone when you do so.

Likewise, there are places where you should speak softly. Did you know that with good vocal energy you can whisper in front of a theater full of people and still be heard? Actors in live theater do it all the time; it's called a *stage whisper*. Stage whispers are even easier to do with a microphone. All you do is lower your volume to just above the level you'd use in a real whisper and lean into the microphone a bit. Aside from some of the obvious places ("After the fire there was a quiet whisper"), a near-whisper is very effective in proclaiming murmurings and subversion and seductions. Be sure to keep your vocal energy up even in a whisper; direct your whisper toward the whole community.

Work on varying your loudness with the following passage. Raise your voice as Jesus calls out to Zacchaeus; soften your voice to a stage whisper to speak the grumblings of the crowd:

> When Jesus came to the place, he looked up and said to him,
>
> "Zacchaeus, hurry and come down;
>
> for I must stay at your house today."
>
> So he hurried down and was happy to welcome him.
>
> All who saw it began to grumble and said,
>
> "He has gone to be the guest of one who is a sinner."
>
> (Luke 19:5–6 NRSV; Ordinary 31C[1])

Another aspect of vocal energy is having enough volume to be heard. Even though you will generally be working with a microphone (see "Wired for Sound," pages 45–47), a microphone doesn't do all the work. You still need to project sufficiently. You should also be able to project well enough to proclaim in small spaces without a microphone.

Projection involves two factors: air and placement. *Air* refers to the amount of air you inhale and the pressure with which you exhale. The more air you have, the more flexibility you have in your volume and in how long you can speak without pausing for another breath.

There are a few different breathing techniques for projection. The one that is familiar to most actors is called *diaphragmatic breathing*, or "breathing through your stomach." Now, of course, you can't literally breathe through your stomach,

---

1. Proper 26C.

but the phrase is a reminder to use your diaphragm, the muscle that stretches across the bottom of your rib cage between your chest and your gut. Slowly stick out your stomach as you inhale; this stretches the diaphragm and allows you to take more air into your lungs. Inhale deeply, as though you were actually pulling air all the way down to your stomach. Then, as you exhale, contract your stomach to force the air out of your windpipe. Breathing this way as you proclaim gives you more volume and vocal energy, even when you speak softly.

Wired for Sound

Every so often, "old-school" actors will complain about how amplified sound has ruined the theater. "In my day," they'll declare, "I could reach the top row of the third balcony with nothing more than a whisper." It's true that, when all the actors are wearing microphones, somehow a performance seems less "live." But thanks to the influence of movies, television, and rock concerts, electronically amplified sound is a permanent part of most theater today.

In the same way, except for proclamations in small spaces, almost every proclaimer uses a microphone. (It would be an interesting experiment to get rid of the microphones in some churches, and require lectors and presiders to work on really projecting. I suspect liturgy would become much more intimate. For one thing, it would make sitting in the back of church far less attractive!) Working with a microphone is a skill, and just like any other skill, it takes practice. Find opportunities to practice with the microphone set up in your community's worship space. Whether in your home community or not, the following tips can help you get the most out of the mic.

There are two kinds of microphones: *omnidirectional* and *unidirectional*. You don't need to be able to distinguish between the two other than to know that some microphones (unidirectional) only pick up sound from directly in front of them, while others (omnidirectional) pick up sound both from in front and from the side. That said, individual mics of either type vary greatly in their sensitivity; some will require you to almost swallow them to be heard while others will produce a distorted sound if you're closer than six inches.

This means a sound check should always be part of your preparation, especially in a new space. Even in a space you've worked in before, it's a good idea to do a sound check as levels can sometimes be changed without your knowledge. Doing at least a perfunctory check before worship starts will save you from surprises when you reach the ambo.

Although you can do a sound check by yourself, it's better to have someone in the worship space listening for you. The ambo is usually not the best place to judge the sound heard in the rest of the space.

The two components that determine sound quality are position of the microphone relative to your mouth and the volume of your voice. The best position for a microphone is . . . where you can be heard! In general, however, most mics work best about four to six inches from your mouth. Since you will be glancing up to make eye contact with the community (see the next chapter) and down to read the text, be sure to position the mic with your head in the "glance down" position. If you position it while your head is up in the "eye contact" position, your mouth may be too close to the mic when you glance down.

Finding the best position for the mic is trial-and-error. If your community has a sound engineer, then let that person instruct you. Otherwise, you and your associate will have to work on it. Some mics work best if they are positioned *on-axis*—that is, pointing directly at your mouth. However, this placement can increase the "popping" sound that comes from air hitting the mic when you pronounce the letters p, b, d, or t. These are known as plosive consonants because they are formed by a short puff of air from your mouth. If the mic set-up allows it, you can reduce this by placing the mic *off-axis*, that is, slightly off to one side, so you're speaking across the mic, or by pointing it at your chin.

Check the sound by using your proclamation rather than something like "Check, one, two." You're more likely to get a realistic check that way. Be sure to use the volume that you will use during worship, and glance up and down to make eye contact. Ask your associate to check your sound level. Have this person move all around the space and check levels from all areas, especially if there are any areas where it's particularly hard to hear. Your associate should tell you not only whether you are loud enough but also whether you are distinct enough. A sound system that carries your voice loudly but distorts it, even slightly, is just as bad as one that is not loud enough at all. If you are not loud enough, you may need to move the mic closer to or more in front of your mouth. If you are too loud, or if the sound is distorted, you may need to move the mic farther away, stand farther away from the mic, or lower your volume.

If you have to pull the mic closer or position it more in front of your mouth, be aware that this will increase the tendency for your plosive consonants to pop.

If you've seen radio announcers or singers in a recording studio as they work, you may have noticed a little screen placed between their mouth and the mike. That's a *pop screen*, and it's designed to stop the air on their plosives and eliminate that pop.

You won't be able to work with such a screen, but you can try to reduce the amount of air you expel when you pronounce plosives. This takes a lot of practice. To try it, hold your hand directly in front of your mouth and speak. Whenever you pronounce a plosive, you'll feel a puff of air hit your hand. See if you can pull back your airflow a bit on your plosives and reduce the air that hits your hand. It's not easy, but it can be done. The other option is to be conscious of where these plosives are in your reading, especially p's, and pull back from the mic a bit when you get to them.

This is also a good time to check whether you're reading too fast or too slow. As I've pointed out, churches often have poor acoustics. Ironically, churches built before the advent of electronic sound systems were designed with architectural features to amplify sound (the use of marble, the "clamshell" hovering over the pulpit, the high arch or half dome over the sanctuary). These churches are considered *live spaces* by a sound engineer because a sound tends to echo or hang in the air before dying out. Unfortunately, once a sound system is installed in such places, the architecture competes with the electronic system, and the result is even more echo that distorts the spoken word, often to the point of rendering it unintelligible. Slowing down helps to reduce this effect. Your associate can check to see if you are competing with your own echo by reading too fast.

Once you discover the best position for the mic, make a mental note of where it is so you can quickly adjust the mic to that position again. Don't be timid about moving the mic. Many gooseneck mics or mic holders make a noise when they're moved. Move them anyway, unless you're told specifically not to (in which case you *must* do a sound check to determine where you need to position yourself and how loud you have to be). The community will no doubt be used to this noise, and it's far better to have a momentary screech than to leave the mic in a position that ensures your proclamation can't be heard.

You'll also want to remember to adjust your distance from the mic when you change your volume in the reading. When you get loud, move a bit farther away; when you get soft, move a bit closer.

If you're tall and you can't get the mic close enough to your mouth, work on projecting at a greater volume rather than leaning down to get closer to the mic. A hunched posture is not very open to the community. Besides, you will be able to make eye contact more easily if you stand up straight. On the other hand, if you are shorter than the mic, arrange for something to stand on so you don't have to crane your neck to get close to it.

An empty space handles sound differently than a full one. You know, for example, that a church full of people echoes less than an empty one because human bodies (and their clothes and coats) are great sound absorbers. Thus, you may have to increase your volume somewhat during the actual proclamation to compensate for the absorbed sound. Ask someone in the community to give you feedback on how well you could be heard during your proclamation.

 To test whether you're doing this correctly, place your hand on your stomach and make a *ha* sound repeatedly. You should feel your stomach expand with each in-breath and contract with each *ha*. If not, then you are breathing from your chest.

The second element to projection is *placement*. Some of us, when we speak, place our voice in the back of our throat. This is fine for everyday conversation, but it's easier to project when we place our voice more forward. This placement allows our sinuses and the bones of our head and face to act as natural resonators and amplify our voice. Diction and clarity usually improve as well because a forward voice is more distinct. This is why, although diaphragmatic breathing isn't absolutely required when working with a microphone, correct placement is.

To experiment with the placement of your voice, open your mouth and say *ahhh*. (Don't stick out your tongue. This isn't a doctor's office!) Keep the *ahhh* sound going, and close your lips so you're kind of humming. Take a breath as needed. Now move the sound forward in your head (by changing the shape of your cheeks and tongue) until you feel the vibration strongly in your lips. You may also feel the vibration in your nose, cheeks, and the bones of your skull. Once you feel this, open your mouth again and hear the difference in the *ahhh* sound from what you started with.

If you have trouble with this exercise, try making an *ng* sound. Say the phrase "dinging, pinging, ringing, singing," and really emphasize the *ng* sounds as you do. Make them sound very nasal. You should feel the sound vibrate in your nose and sinuses. Place your hand on your face and feel the vibration. Start with the *ng* sound, and then, keeping your voice in the same place, change to an *ahhh* sound. See if you can still feel the vibrations.

Another way to practice placing sound forward is to imagine that you are trying to hit an object across the room with a short *ha* sound. Trying to "throw" the sound across the room will force you to place the sound more forward in your head. This is also a good exercise to help you project your vocal energy.

Don't worry too much if you don't get this right away. Vocal energy and projection are tough to learn even for some actors. It's been said that microphones make for lazy actors (and singers), but even with a mic, your effectiveness as a proclaimer will be enhanced if you can learn to project as well.

Inflection

Inflection is the melody of speech. It refers to how high and low our voice goes (its pitch) as we speak. We convey much through inflection. By raising our inflection at the end of a sentence, for example, we turn it into a question. Inflection also conveys attitude. When her teenager says, "I'll be happy to take out the garbage," Mom either responds, "Thanks" or "Don't use that tone of voice with me!" depending on the inflection in her child's voice.

Everyone has a range of inflection in their speech. The wider the range, the more expressive the speech. Someone who spoke in a monotone would be said to have no range of inflection at all. Radio, television, or sports announcers might exaggerate their inflection by running from the bottom of their range to the top. We use the extremes of our range when we're excited or angry or passionate, as these extremes show great energy and emotion. Listen to people tell stories with passion and feeling—their voices go up and down the scale as they convey their excitement.

 Something strange happens, though, to many lectors when they proclaim the Word of God. They tend to limit their range severely and vary their inflection very little. They're like artists who, though they have a palette of twenty-five or thirty colors to choose from, use only five or six. The result is a reading that's bland and unexpressive.

Some lectors feel that the reading of the Word of God calls for a steady, formal tone; speaking without much inflection sounds to them more serious, even divine. But there are many ways to express the sacred. Restorers were quite surprised when, after removing centuries of dirt and candle soot from the ceiling of the Sistine Chapel, they found that Michelangelo had used very vibrant and powerful colors in his paintings. What was once a serious, muted room has come alive in a manner consistent with the artist's intent. How many of us add a layer of soot to the colors of Scripture when we proclaim without using the full range of our inflection?

Practice expanding your range of inflection with the following passage. This is exhortation, so most of it should be proclaimed in the upper range of your inflection. Try going higher than you usually do when proclaiming, at least for the purpose of this exercise. Raise your inflection even higher on the underlined words:

> On that day, it shall be said to Jerusalem:
>> Fear not, O Zion, be not discouraged!
> The LORD, your God, is in your midst,
>> a mighty savior;
> he will rejoice over you with gladness,
>> and renew you in his love,
> he will sing joyfully because of you,
>> as one sings at festivals.   (Zephaniah 3:16–18a; Advent 3C)

You may choose to vary your inflection elsewhere; just be sure to make some variations. You'll notice, too, that inflection is closely tied to rhythm, because we often raise our inflection on syllables that we stress. (We also tend to increase our vocal energy when we raise our inflection.) Speaking the text casually, as suggested in the last chapter, will give you a feel for inflection. Also, identifying choice words will help you find places to vary your inflection.

If you don't think you have a wide range of inflection in your everyday voice, then strive to broaden it. Americans generally speak with a narrower range of inflection than, say, the British, Spanish, or Italians. But you can work on improving it and giving yourself a broad palette of colors for your proclamation. Pay attention, for example, to your range of inflection when you're speaking about your favorite sports team, your hobby, or your children or grandchildren. You may be surprised at how much you vary your inflection when you speak of the things you care most about. Use that same range to speak with passion about these texts.

Dying Inflection

Before we leave our discussion on voice, I need to point out another problem inherent in American speech, called the *dying inflection*. Just as we indicate a query by raising our inflection at the end of a question, we indicate a statement by dropping our inflection at the end of a sentence. This is a clue to our listener that we've completed a thought and it's okay to stop listening. If we start a new statement, we must raise our vocal energy again to regain their attention.

Listen for this yourself in a conversation. If in the course of conversation, you have something to say, you listen for a dying inflection and a slight pause before jumping in. But if the speaker wishes to "top" you and prevent you from speaking, it requires that the speaker continue quickly and with a boost of vocal energy. It's not rude (well, not always); it's just the way our conversations flow in American speech. But when we transfer that tendency to proclamation, it becomes a problem.

If you use a dying inflection at the end of every sentence, or worse, within sentences at the conclusion of a thought (at each pause, perhaps), then you're giving your community permission to "check out" and stop listening. The effect may be subconscious, but it makes it difficult for them to stay attentive. If you drop your energy at the end of each thought, you have to bump it up again at the start of the next line. It's like driving down a long street with a stop sign at each block. The start and stop in your vocal energy makes for a disconnected reading that requires more effort to understand.

Be mindful of this in your proclamation. When you pause at a minor break in thought (at a comma or at the end of a sense line), keep your voice *up* so your listeners know that you're not finished and that the next thought is connected. Think of the commas as little "up arrows," which are there to remind you to keep your vocal energy and inflection up. You will find that some readings, especially from Paul's epistles, contain one continuous thought all the way through, so keep your voice up until you finish.

Of course, you have to use a dying inflection when you conclude a significant thought; that's one of the rules of communication. But be sure you use it only at the *very* end, and don't drop your inflection too much or you'll swallow the last word. Be especially careful when important words (choice words) occur at the end of a phrase or line. Dropping your energy and inflection on these words will make it difficult for your community to understand you.

Read this passage and try to inflect up at the end of each phrase:

> God made the two great lights,
>   the greater one to govern the day,
>   and the lesser one to govern the night;
>   and he made the stars.
> God set them in the dome of the sky,
>   to shed light upon the earth,
>   to govern the day and the night,
>   and to separate the light from the darkness.   (Genesis 1:16–18)

 Be especially conscious of the addresses that open many readings: "Beloved," "Brothers and sisters," "Thus says the LORD," "Jesus said to his disciples." Keeping your voice *up* at the end of these introductions will make your community eager to hear what comes next!

Practicing the Scales

Don't be overly concerned with finding the "correct" tempo, rhythm, volume, or inflection for every text you proclaim. Why? Because much of this will flow naturally from the interpretation of the text. When you proclaim fully, you give the community more than just the words; you give them the message beyond the words. Effective proclamation—our goal—includes both verbal and non-verbal cues (as does everyday conversation), and their combination makes it much easier for a community to understand the text.

As we noted at the beginning of this chapter, a lector's work on voice, like an actor's, is just a starting point. We would never limit our preparation to voice work alone and then go out and proclaim. No, rather, this work is our version of the scales Paderewski practiced each day. No one ever paid to see him play scales at a concert, but his practice ensured that whatever he did play in concert was that much better. After moving on to the work in subsequent chapters, you may want to return here from time to time to check that you haven't forgotten about or become careless with some of these basic elements of proclamation.

Eight Important Things to Remember about Voice

1. Read slowly, especially when you're new to the ministry of lector. Slow down even more when you're in a space that produces a lot of echo. In general, if you think you're reading too slowly, you're probably reading just right.

2. Use rhythm to make sure your reading is understood. Stress the comparative words in parallel constructions and paradoxes.

3. Use pauses to convey meaning. Pause in order to
   ✤ break up separate thoughts
   ✤ set apart significant statements
   ✤ indicate major shifts in the text

4. Don't pause in the middle of a single thought.

5. Project your vocal energy to connect with everyone in the space. Link your vocal energy with eye contact.

6. Vary your volume as appropriate.

7. Use a wide range of inflection to bring color and variety to your proclamation.

8. Keep your voice up at pauses and at the end of phrases, dropping it slightly only at the very end of a thought.

Chapter 4

Working on Physicalization: The Ambo Is Not a Radio

It's interesting that, very soon after texting became practical, people began introducing symbols (called *emoticons* or *emojis*) to convey additional meaning that was not evident in the words. Many of these emojis represent various facial expressions, as if users were trying to "show" their faces to their recipients so that nuances of meaning could be communicated. The rapidity with which emojis became a natural part of our text conversations demonstrates the intuitive need we have for visual, bodily clues to meaning.

If our goal as lectors is to ensure that our communities understand the full meaning of the text we proclaim, then we must provide these clues as well.

It's true that the most important asset for actors is their voice, but their second-most important asset is their body. Think of all that actors convey through their bodies, especially their faces and eyes. An actor's look and posture can convey even more than the lines spoken. Many of the most powerful moments in film and theater happen without any words at all. The same is true in our everyday lives: a touch, a hug, a glance, a roll of the eyes, a turn toward or a turn away, standing up tall, or slouching over—all of these say a great deal without saying anything. In fact, we communicate much more nonverbally than we do with words.

Thus if we're just using our voice in proclaiming Scripture, and not using our bodies as well, we're only giving our communities half the story and communicating only halfway. Truth be told, we *are* communicating with our bodies whether we are conscious of it or not. When we read hunched over the lectionary, never looking up, with a death grip on the ambo, intent only on *reading* the text, we are, in fact, saying something: we're saying that we think these Scriptures are boring, stolid, fossilized texts that we are either unworthy or unprepared to proclaim. That's not exactly the message we want to convey. In order for the assembly to be actively engaged in these stories, we need to actively invite them into the stories with our body language. Let's work, then, on proclaiming not just with our voice but with our entire bodies.

Eye Contact

The first and most important physical element you can add to your proclamation is eye contact. If you're burying your head in the lectionary and never looking at the community, then you might as well be broadcasting your reading over the radio! It's a secret every actor knows: we communicate with our eyes.

Eyes are truly the "window to the soul." When we make eye contact with the community, we connect with them more deeply than with our voice alone. More important, we invite them to connect more deeply to the story we proclaim. This helps the community stay with the story and keeps them involved, which, ideally, makes it less likely their minds will wander or that they will (heaven forbid!) begin reading along in their own missals or Bibles.

All well and good, you might say, but eye contact is pretty hard to maintain when we're reading from a book. How do we look down to read from the lectionary and at the same time look up to make eye contact with the community?

Furthermore, when we first try to make eye contact in our reading, our natural tendency is to look up from the page in the pauses in between phrases and sentences and then go back to the page to read the next phrase. It goes something like this: Look down—read the phrase aloud—pause—look up—look down—read the phrase aloud—pause—look up. But reading this way means we're only making eye contact with our listeners when we're not saying anything. Boring! They're missing out on seeing our eyes when they're the most interesting: when we're actually proclaiming the Word.

 Actors go to great lengths to make sure their eyes can be seen. It's one reason they use makeup when they're onstage. Eyes are where we read emotion, intensity, and spirit. Henry Fonda would never film a close-up without an "inky-dink," a small light placed next to the camera that would shine in his eyes and give them a bright spark. Fonda knew that all his work as an actor would mean little if the audience couldn't connect with his eyes. Our eyes are our most expressive feature. Look at animated characters: their eyes are drawn disproportionately large so we can more easily read their emotions.

We need to work against this tendency so that we look down in the pauses to scan the next phrase and then look up when we read the phrase aloud. This sequence goes like this: Look down—scan the next phrase—look up—proclaim the phrase—pause—look down—scan the next phrase—look up—proclaim the phrase—pause. This is counterintuitive and may feel a bit strange when you first try it, but with repeated practice, it becomes natural.

Try it with this text, (Galatians 3:26–29; Ordinary 12C[1]), which I've divided into sections over the next few pages. Scan the following line once, then look up from the book and say it aloud. See if you remember it correctly.

Through faith you are all children of God in Christ Jesus.

If you didn't get it right the first time, read it over a few times to yourself, and then try it again. It should be easier this time. (This is why repeated practices with the text are important.)

With a longer line, you may need to look down in the middle. Read over the following a few times, and then try to say it without looking.

---

1. Proper 7C.

And if you belong to Christ,
> then you are Abraham's descendant,
> heirs according to the promise.

How far did you get before you had to look down? Try to look down at the natural breaks in lines, in this case, following each comma. As we noted in the last chapter, commas are natural pauses and thus a good place to look down. Read it again, looking down at those points and scanning the rest of the line.

As was also noted in chapter 3, some lectionaries are printed with sense-line divisions so that the lines break at a logical place. These divisions should help you, assuming you are working with a copy that includes the same breaks as the lectionary from which you're proclaiming. If not, you will have to find your own places to break and look down. Always read over the actual text in the lectionary before proclaiming it at liturgy to familiarize yourself with the layout.

The following lines are divided as they appear in the lectionary. Try pausing at the end of each line and scanning the next phrase. Read the text over to yourself first a couple of times to familiarize yourself with it.

> There is neither Jew nor Greek,
> > there is neither slave nor free person,
> > there is not male and female;
> > for you are all one in Christ Jesus.

Remember that we don't always pause at the end of a sense line. Some of the lines need to stay connected to each other to make sense. The following is an example. Although it is broken into two phrases, there is no punctuation at the end of the first phrase, a clue that the first phrase needs to stay connected to the second. Try reading it without pausing; just look down and scan the second phrase as you approach the end of the first.

> For all of you who were baptized into Christ
> > have clothed yourselves with Christ.

Though your goal should be to scan longer and longer phrases, don't do so at the expense of accuracy.

Be aware that literal translations, such as those used as the basis for the Catholic lectionaries in the United States and Canada, contain many convoluted sentence constructions that can be difficult to proclaim. Some of the readings from Paul can be especially challenging. Use caution; if a line is giving you difficulty in practice, make sure you read it directly from the lectionary when you proclaim it.

Now try the whole thing together. See if any lines give you trouble; you might need to read these directly from the text. (Watch for awkward constructions like "all of you who" or "for you are all one." Make sure you get these right.)

Brothers and sisters:

Through faith you are all children of God in Christ Jesus.

For all of you who were baptized into Christ
   have clothed yourselves with Christ.

There is neither Jew nor Greek,
   there is neither slave nor free person,
   there is not male and female;
   for you are all one in Christ Jesus.
   And if you belong to Christ,
   then you are Abraham's descendant,
   heirs according to the promise.

Don't peer down your nose at the text while trying to keep your face forward. At the same time, don't bury your face in the book so the community sees only the top of your head when you glance down. Your head should move only slightly when looking down at the text, but it should move. Keep working at this and it will soon become second nature.

The construction of the ambo can sometimes make this more challenging. The reading surface may not be well lit, shadows may fall across the lectionary, or the microphone may obscure part of the text when you look down. See if moving the book to the right or left eliminates the problem. If the reading surface is very deep, the book might rest so low on it you have to drop your head quite a bit to look down. You might be able to bring the text closer or get it into better light by moving the lectionary up toward the top of the platform, holding it there if necessary, so that you can see the text more easily. If you wear reading glasses or bifocals, you might need to adjust the position of the lectionary accordingly. (You also might not be able to see the assembly clearly when you look up, but that's okay—do it anyway!) As you can see, it's essential you spend some time beforehand familiarizing yourself with the arrangement of the space you'll be proclaiming from, so you can figure out any adjustments you need to make.

Of course, effective eye contact is not simply looking up; rather, you need to look *at* the community when you proclaim.

When you make eye contact with the community, don't always look at the same place. For one thing, the people you're looking at will start to feel uncomfortable! For another, it makes the rest of the community feel ignored and disconnected from you. Spread your eye contact around the community, looking at different places within the assembly area at different points: the left side of the aisle,

 If the thought of looking directly at people while you proclaim makes you nervous, you're in good company; it makes some actors nervous, too. Many famous stage actors have admitted taking comfort in the lights that shine in their eyes because it prevents them from seeing the audience. In your church, you likely don't have bright lights in your eyes shielding your view of the community, so here's a trick you can use: look *just above* the heads of the people in the community. From a distance, it will appear as if you're looking directly at them, but you won't be. Since you won't see them looking back at you, you'll likely be less anxious.

the right side, the side aisles, and so on. Use caution if you have people seated on the sides or behind you. If much of the community is placed there, you'll want to include them occasionally, but swiveling your neck around like an owl while you read is distracting. The best and most inclusive place to look is at the people farthest from you, generally those in the last row of occupied seats. Place your focus there often (but not exclusively) and everyone in front of them will feel included as well. Remember to project your vocal energy along with your eye contact. Direct the energy behind your voice so that it reaches all the way to the people you're looking at.

Eye Lines

Once you've gotten the basics of eye contact down, you may want to use your eyes for more than just connecting with the community. Your eyes can also help the community "see" the story, especially vivid narrative texts or those that include dialogue.

For stories with dialogue, eye placement can help the community keep track of which character is speaking. The trick is very simple: Choose a *focal point* in the worship space for each character who speaks. Focus your eyes on that same spot each time that character speaks. Choose a different spot for each character. Then, every time you look at a certain spot and speak, the community will know which character is speaking. It will also give the illusion that each character sees the other as they are speaking.

A dialogue between two characters is the simplest. One character's focal point should be just to the left of the center of the assembly; the other's should be just to the right of the center. Don't make the focal points so far right or left that you have to crane your neck around to see them. When you look slightly to the left, the community knows it's character A; slightly to the right, it's character B. If you're reading a conversation with three persons, choose a center focal point for character C.

Whenever God speaks directly to someone, resist the temptation to place God's focal point lower than the person God is conversing with, as though God were looking down from heaven to speak. The best focal point for lines spoken by God is straight ahead, into or just over the heads of the community. Likewise, when you address God, don't look up, but look straight into the community.

Choose an actual spot to look at, so each time you look up from the page you can find the spot quickly. Don't be vague: make it the lower corner of the choir loft, or the flower in the St. Thérése window, or the stain on the back wall. Obviously, it will help to get in the space beforehand and work this all out. (If this is impossible, then just let the Spirit guide you. The first time you look up when speaking the character's dialogue, whatever spot your eye hits becomes the focal point.)

Though it may seem complex, this is a basic storytelling convention, and the community will understand it right away. The trick even figures into how dialogue is filmed in a movie. Next time you're watching a scene between two people in a film, notice how in close-ups that show only one actor, one is looking to the right side of the frame and one is looking to the left. When the film cuts between these shots, we more easily understand that these two are speaking to each other. In reality, the close-ups may be shot without the other actor even being present on the set; an assistant director might read the lines off camera. And because equipment might be in way, the actor might not even be looking at the other person but concentrating on a specific focal point (called an "eye line"). So in that scene where the guy says all those tender things to the girl, he may actually be looking adoringly at an X on a piece of tape while talking to a man with donut crumbs in his beard!

Practice the technique using the following text. In this passage, most of the dialogue belongs to Samuel, so use a focal point to the left or right of center for him. Make it the side that will include most of the community; for example, if most of the community is assembled to the right of the ambo, then make Samuel's focal point to the right. Use a point straight ahead for God's words. Then, in Samuel's conversation with Jesse, keep Samuel's focal point the same as before, and make Jesse's point the opposite side. For the narrative sections, vary your focus, remembering to take in as much of the community as possible.

> The LORD said to Samuel:
>> "Fill your horn with oil, and be on
>>> your way.
>> I am sending you to Jesse of Bethlehem,
>>> for I have chosen my king from among
>>>> his sons."
>> As Jesse and his sons came to the sacrifice,
>>> Samuel looked at Eliab and thought,
>>> "Surely the Lord's anointed is here
>>>> before him."
> But the LORD said to Samuel:
>> "Do not judge from his appearance
>>> or from his lofty stature,
>> because I have rejected him.
>> Not as man sees does God see,
>>> because man sees the appearance
>>> but the LORD looks into the heart."
> In the same way Jesse presented seven
>> sons before Samuel,
>> but Samuel said to Jesse,
>>> "The LORD has not chosen any one
>>>> of these."
> Then Samuel asked Jesse,
>> "Are these all the sons you have?"
> Jesse replied,
>> "There is still the youngest, who is
>>> tending the sheep."
> Samuel said to Jesse,
>> "Send for him;
>> we will not begin the sacrificial
>>> banquet until he arrives here."
> Jesse sent and had the young man brought
>> to them.
> He was ruddy, a youth handsome to
>> behold
>> and making a splendid appearance.
> The LORD said,
>> "There—anoint him, for this is the one!"
> Then Samuel, with the horn of oil in hand,
>> anointed David in the presence of his
>>> brothers;
>> and from that day on, the spirit of the
>>> Lord rushed upon David.
>>>> (1 Samuel 16:1b, 6–7, 10–13a; Lent 4A)

These techniques take practice, so give yourself permission to start out slowly until you get used to it. Keep working at it until you can be in eye contact with the community for about seventy-five percent of your reading. At the very least, try to make eye contact at the important lines—especially at any choice words.

Body Position

Hands are great nonverbal communicators, so as lectors we need to be aware of their potential and their challenge. First, there are a few things you should *not* be doing with your hands when you read.

I recommend that you not hold your place in the text with your finger. Some lectors do this to make sure they don't lose their place when they look up to make eye contact. While their intention is correct, I still recommend against the practice; it can be distracting to the community. If you absolutely need to do it to be comfortable making eye contact, then do it, but if you practice your reading enough beforehand, it may not be necessary.

Don't stand at the ambo with your hands down at your side or, worse, clasped behind you. This posture appears overly casual and physically separates you from the ambo and the Word itself. On the other hand, don't stand ramrod straight, which conveys a very cold, authoritarian, unwelcoming spirit that distances you from the community.

The strongest and best stance is a relaxed posture, feet about shoulder-width apart, with your hands resting on the sides of ambo or on the lectionary itself. Rest them in a relaxed state, not in a wrestler's grip. This physical connection with the text you are proclaiming gives the community the sense that you're at ease with and "grounded" in the Word you are proclaiming. Once you're in this position at the ambo, don't move about, rock back and forth, fidget, or shift your weight repeatedly from foot to foot.

A relaxed, open, grounded stance engages the attention of the community, and strengthens the impact of your proclamation. It's also the best posture to support your voice.

The Secret Ingredient

There is one simple and incredibly effective physicalization that you can employ as a proclaimer. In fact, it's the secret ingredient I use whenever I have little time to train lectors because its effect is so pronounced. Let me show you how to use it.

As you prepare your reading, ask yourself, "Is what I am proclaiming good news or bad news?" I don't mean good news in the sense of *gospel*; in that sense, all of Scripture is good news, telling of God's marvelous love for us. But is the specific piece of Scripture you're reading good news in its own context? Some texts are not—for example, the rebukes of the prophets or the lamentations over the suffering of God's people. Even the Passion in its own context is violent, ugly news.

But apart from these instances, much of Scripture is good news, especially much of what we hear on Sundays. It tells of God's great love, mercy, forgiveness, and compassion. That's really good news, so when you're proclaiming these Scriptures, why not do what you would do in your own life when you share good news—*smile*!

You'd be amazed how much a simple smile can change your whole demeanor, even your voice. If you don't believe it, record yourself saying something mundane (your outgoing voicemail message is a good choice). First, record it in a normal, flat voice and play it back. Then record it again, and change nothing,

First Looks

For an actor, an audition is a job interview, so actors work very hard honing their audition skills. It's very important to start off strong in an audition, because directors will probably decide within the first thirty seconds whether they are interested or not. The same principle applies in reading. If you fail to engage the community right away, it will be difficult or impossible to catch up later on. Your mother was right: First impressions are important.

Put some thought into how you start. In fact, put some thought into what you do before you start. Actors know they are auditioning from the moment they walk into the room to meet the director. How do you walk up to the ambo? How do you carry yourself as you adjust the lectionary or the microphone? What does your very first look at the assembly say? While you're doing all this, the assembly is watching and making judgments. It's not right or wrong; it's simply human nature. They are deciding: Is this man comfortable in his ministry? Is this woman confident, assured, and present to her task? Basically, they're asking, "Is this person worth listening to?"

Be aware that there is a trap at the very start of each reading that could cause you to lose the attention of assembly: the announcement "A reading from the Book of So-and-So." If you're diligent about eye contact, you announce this while looking at the assembly, and then look down to scan the first phrase of the reading and look up again to proclaim it. However, that brief moment of broken eye contact at the beginning of the reading will be enough for many in the community to lose you (and, if the text is available, start reading along themselves).

This is akin to the situation in auditions in which actors announce their name, their agent's name, or the name of their audition piece, and then pause and start the audition. Let me share a trick I was taught to avoid this trap: *memorize the first line of your reading* (not the whole thing, just the first line or phrase). Then you can pause after the announcement and start the reading without breaking eye contact with the community.

Your "opening moves" might go something like this:

1. Approach the ambo with reverence. Don't rush up, but don't walk like you're in a funeral procession either.

2. If necessary, adjust the microphone or the lectionary as discreetly as possible. Stand in a relaxed posture. Place your hands in a neutral position on the ambo or lectionary.

3. Look down and scan the "A reading from . . ." line and the first phrase of the reading to refresh your memory. Take a deep the breath to calm yourself.

4. Look up and take in the entire community with your glance.

5. Announce the reading and then pause, without looking back down and losing eye contact with the community. While maintaining eye contact, proclaim the first phrase of the reading

6. Then look down, scan the next phrase, and continue the reading. You're on your way.

except this time smile when you speak. Play it back and you'll notice that you can actually "hear" the smile in your voice. (Leave the message that way and you might even encourage your callers to smile back in the messages they leave!)

Once, when I recommended to a lector that he try rereading the text he was practicing and adding a smile, he responded that he had recently had jaw surgery and couldn't! A bit embarrassed, I told him he needn't try again, but he insisted, and the change was amazing: he smiled with his eyes, his voice, his body, his energy, conveying the excitement of the good news he was proclaiming.

I'm not suggesting you paste a fake "game show host" smile on your face the whole time. Some readings aren't good news all the way through. But you can smile when you get to the good parts. Your smile will come naturally as you share the good news. That's why it's important to pray with and reflect on these texts. If you don't, you won't know where the good parts are! As Pope Francis reminds us, "an evangelizer must never look like someone who has just come back from a funeral!"[2]

If you still have trouble with this or think that smiling is not appropriate from the ambo, try it once. Practice using Paul's great exhortation to the Philippians:

> Brothers and sisters:
>
> Rejoice in the Lord always.
>
> I shall say it again: rejoice!
>
> Your kindness should be known to all.
>
> The Lord is near.
>
> Have no anxiety at all, but in everything,
>
>> by prayer and petition, with thanksgiving,
>>
>> make your requests known to God.
>
> Then the peace of God that surpasses all understanding
>
>> will guard your hearts and minds in Christ Jesus.
>
> (Philippians 4:4–7; Advent 3C)

Can't you hear the smile in Paul's voice as he wrote this? Don't you think that the Philippians were smiling when they heard it? If you aren't smiling when you read it, if you yourself aren't doing the very thing you're calling on the community to do, are you really being truthful to the Word that you proclaim?

Go Organic

Actors and directors use the word *organic* to describe acting that is truthful and that flows from the text and the characters in it. Physical and emotional expressions seem real when they grow *from* the text rather than when they are forced *onto* it. The same is true in proclamation. Physicalization must flow from the text first. Don't try to force a smile where it doesn't belong. Even eye contact flows from the rhythm of the text.

In the same way, however, reading a text without any physicalization robs it of its truest expression. If you're uncomfortable with some of the techniques in this chapter, work on giving yourself permission to tell the stories of our faith with the same vigor that you tell the stories of your life. After all, the Word of God deserves to be served by all of your communication talent, including these nonverbal skills.

---

2. *Evangelii gaudium*, 10.

Four Important Things to Remember about Physicalization

1. Make eye contact frequently with the community, glancing down when pausing and up when proclaiming.

2. Include everyone in the community with your glance, looking most often at or just above the people who are farthest away.

3. Stand at the ambo or lectern in a relaxed, open posture, hands on the lectionary or on the ambo.

4. Smile when you read good news!

Chapter 5

Working on Intention: We All Have Our Own Isaiah

There's a clichéd story about the actor who, being told to do some stage business or movement by the director, asks, "What's my motivation?" The director replies, "Your paycheck!"

This story pokes fun at actors who must find a motivation for every single thing their characters do or say or even think about, but, in truth, we rarely do much in our lives without a specific reason. Thus, whether it's called *motivation* or *action* or *intention*, actors spend a lot of time seeking to understand what drives their characters. Only with such an understanding can they bring the characters to believable life.

Intention

Ritual is *purposeful action*. Everything we do in ritual has a purpose or intention. Our readings are no exception. As stories, they have their own intentions. There is a reason that these stories were told. Their authors had specific intentions in composing them, the storytellers had specific intentions in retelling them, and the editors of Scripture and of the lectionary had specific intentions for including them in their canon. As proclaimers, it's our responsibility to uncover these intentions and make them our own. Otherwise, we read without purpose.

Reading without purpose is a dangerous trap for lectors. Ask some lectors why they read and they might answer, "Because it's time," or "Because I was told to," or "Just because that's what we do." When we read without a purpose, we lose the *need to communicate*.

This need is what drives most of our everyday communication. If we have a very strong need to communicate, then we work especially hard to be understood. For example, we work harder to communicate our love to someone than we do to tell them about a funny video we saw. For our proclamation to be effective, we have to rediscover our need to communicate; we have to rediscover our *intention*.

Intention answers the question why: Why are you saying what you're saying? Intention gives the thrust to the reading. In speaking of the importance of Scripture study for lectors, the introduction to the *Lectionary for Mass* says, "The purpose of their biblical formation is to give readers the ability to understand the readings in context and to perceive by the light of faith *the central point of the revealed message*."[1] This point is intention.

It's interesting to note that the creators of the lectionary assign the lector the responsibility for perceiving what the intention of the reading is, and are confident that the Spirit will provide the light of faith to do so. This means that the central point of each reading cannot be predetermined and given in the lectionary. Thus, different lectors may come up with different intentions. Is this permissible? Isn't this interpretation, and aren't lectors discouraged from interpreting Scripture?

Why do actors keep playing Hamlet? Surely there have been enough Hamlets in the world. In fact, after the first one, why would anyone bother to do it again? Well, I guess there were a lot of people outside of seventeenth-century London who never saw that first Hamlet. Fair enough. But now we have film. After Kenneth Branaugh or Lawrence Olivier's award-winning performance, why would we watch someone else do it again? It's not like there will be fewer corpses at the end!

The reason, of course, that we keep watching *Hamlet* and will keep watching *Hamlet* is because each actor brings a different interpretation to the role. With every different performance we learn something more about Hamlet that we didn't know before. My mother read *War and Peace* at least three times. She said that each time she felt and learned something different about the characters. That's part of the genius of Shakespeare and other great writers; no one performance or reading can really plumb the depths of their characters.

Can we say less about Scripture? Scripture is so rich, so deep, that any single interpretation will always be incomplete. The same piece of Scripture can have a profoundly different effect on different people; it can even have a different effect on the same person at different times in the course of that person's life. The Protestant tradition, following the lead of Martin Luther, has always put forth this understanding of Scripture. The Catholic tradition has recognized that, even in liturgy, "The Spirit also brings home to each person individually everything that in the proclamation of the word of God is spoken for the good of the whole gathering of the faithful. In strengthening the unity of all, the Holy Spirit at the same time fosters a diversity of gifts and furthers their multiform operation."[2]

The intention I choose, then, will be influenced by my life, my culture, my community, my prayer, and my study. It may be as different from the intention you choose as your life, culture, community, prayer, and study are different from mine. My proclamation of Isaiah not only will be, but *should be*, different from yours. I am a part of the Body of Christ just as you are a part. My right and responsibility to choose an intention comes from my being baptized into the Body of Christ, just as yours does. My entire ministry flows from that baptism, in fact.

---

1. Introduction, *Lectionary for Mass*, 55; emphasis is mine.
2. Introduction, *Lectionary for Mass*, 9.

Thus, my Isaiah and your Isaiah are part of the "diversity of gifts" in the Body of Christ and evidence of their "multiform operation." If it were not so, then we should pick the one person in our community who we think does the best interpretation of Isaiah and have that person always proclaim the readings from that prophet.

Being exposed to only one viewpoint is not only boring, it's bad theology. If we truly proclaim that we are the Body of Christ, and that we all have our unique gifts and perspective for building up that Body (1 Corinthians 12:7), then we should celebrate that diversity of gifts and not look to homogenize everyone.

Remember, you never know how you and your choice might speak to someone in a way that no one else could speak. Your particular choice could be just the one that someone in your community needs to hear on the day you proclaim it.

Yet it's right to be cautious about interpretation. Scripture has been used over the centuries (and is still used today) to justify some pretty horrendous things: war, slavery, segregation, the subjugation of women, economic injustice, capital punishment, and other travesties we'd prefer to forget. We do well not to forget them, however, because they remind us that we interpret Scripture as we are: imperfect creatures prone to mistakes. This doesn't mean we don't undertake the challenge, but that we do so humbly and put all our work under the guidance of the Spirit and the inherited wisdom of the Church. This is another reason why a life infused with prayer and study of Scripture is so essential to the ministry of a lector.

Choosing an Intention

Let's practice identifying intention. Consider this passage from Paul's Letter to the Romans:

> Brothers and sisters:
> None of us lives for oneself, and no one dies for oneself.
> For if we live, we live for the Lord,
> > and if we die, we die for the Lord;
> > so then, whether we live or die, we are the Lord's.
> For this is why Christ died and came to life,
> > that he might be Lord of both the dead and the living.
>
> (Romans 14:7–9; Ordinary 24A[3])

What is Paul trying to say? Why is he writing this to the Romans? A check of what comes before and after in chapter 14 shows that this excerpt is from a longer passage in which Paul warns the Romans not to judge each other's behavior.[4] The verse following this excerpt says, for example, "Why do you pass judgment on your brother or sister? Or you, why do you despise your brother or sister?" (NRSV). One possible reason Paul wrote this was to tell the Romans to stop judging each other.

3. Proper 19A

4. The *Revised Common Lectionary* excerpt includes most of these verses.

But the excerpt taken by itself presents other possibilities. Emphasizing the unity of all Christians, including those who have died, Paul's intention could be to have the Romans end their divisions. The line "whether we live or die, we are the Lord's" reflects Paul's assertion throughout Romans that we belong to God. So Paul may have written this to drive home this point and give the Romans hope.

Which intention is correct? The answer is *whichever one you choose.* All of these, and more, are justified by the text, either in context or by itself. How do you choose? Well, that's up to you and the Spirit. Your choice may be whichever one speaks to you, whichever one you believe the community most needs to hear, or whichever one you feel the text most implies. Go back to some of the notes you made at your first reading; you'll be surprised at how often your intention is right there in your first impressions. Take the text into prayer, and ask for the Spirit's guidance in your choice. "Prayer should accompany the reading of sacred Scripture, so that a dialogue takes place between God and man."[5]

Why not also ask the author of the text for guidance as well? While praying with the saints is an idea most Catholics are comfortable with, all Christians believe in the *communion of saints,* both living and dead. (It's in our common creed.) If you were uncertain about a passage in a book, wouldn't you ask the author about it if you had the opportunity? Well, you do have the opportunity, because the author, Paul, is still a member of the Body of Christ!

Usually, one intention will emerge for you as you prepare the readings, especially as you pray with them. If you discern multiple possible intentions, then let the contexts be your guide. Consider which intention might be consonant with the overall intention of the Scriptures the excerpt is taken from. Consider the context of the other readings for that Sunday, if your reading is complementary. (Actually, this one is not.) What is their intention? Can you choose an intention that is complementary? What about the context of the season? If the reading belongs to Easter Time, Christmas Time, Lent, or Advent, consider an intention that coordinates with the character of that season. What about the readings from the previous or following weeks? Is there a consistent intention being put forward over these weeks?

Let's say that, for this reading, we choose the intention that Paul wants to give the Romans hope. Phrase the intention in terms of what Paul wants: "Paul wants the Romans to hope," or, even better, as a command from Paul: "Be hopeful!" The other intentions could also be phrased this way: "Be unified!" "Stop judging each other!" Do you see how this gives strength to the reading? If we were to proclaim the reading with that one thought in our heads through the whole proclamation, it would take on an energy and immediacy it might not have had before. This is why actors love the power of intention.

---

5. *Dei Verbum,* 25.

But there's one more change to the intention we need to make before we proclaim. Instead of thinking of the central message of the proclamation as "Paul wants the Romans to be hopeful," we must recast the message as "I want *you* to be hopeful."

This is not to say that you pretend that you are Paul and that your community is Rome, or that you are Jeremiah and your community is Israel, or that you are Matthew and your community is a group of first-century Christians. Doing such pretending is often what leads to the dreaded "performance" in a reading. We aren't recreating a proclamation that happened two thousand years ago. We are proclaiming anew a theme that has resounded for two thousand years. Storytellers don't create new stories, but neither do they simply repeat word-for-word stories that they have heard. They add their own nuances to the story for the benefit of their present audience.

Thus, you need to cast yourself as the proclaimer of a message that Paul originally delivered to the Romans because they needed to hear it, but which *you* are now delivering to *your community* because *your community* needs to hear it. There is always an immediate need for story, even if it is to remind us of who we are before too much time passes and we begin to forget. As Sam points out in *Avalon*, when you stop remembering, you forget.

So as you proclaim the message, it is a message to the community today. Your intention is the *why* that brings you to the ambo to proclaim. Your whole reason for proclaiming is to say, "Hope! I want you, people of this community, to hope. Here are words of hope, written for *you*!"

Are You Talking to Me?

Have you noticed something about people who live in commercials? First, no one has a dysfunctional family. Second, all husbands are inept but their wives love them for it. And most important, you, the viewer, are always such a good friend of the spokespersons that they are going to let you in on all their housekeeping/automotive/financial/fresh breath secrets.

Many actors are very successful in commercials because they can look right into the camera and make you feel like they are talking only to you. They have mastered the technique of *specificity*.

It's very hard to talk to people in general. We don't really have any practice doing so. All day long, we talk to specific people in our lives—our coworkers, spouse, children, friends—and we speak differently to each of them. Listen to someone tell a story, or be conscious of yourself sometime, and see how we make subtle changes in our telling based on who we're speaking to. How can we use this natural ability when we speak in front of a community?

Most of us know how to keep people's attention when we're in an everyday conversation. We're engaging speakers in our daily lives. But put us in front of a group, with no one to make any direct responses, and we go flat. Actors have the same problem when they are given monologues to perform. While most training for actors involves scenes with at least one other person, occasionally actors are required to speak directly to the audience in an aside or monologue.

The way to keep these moments as engaging as the ones in a scene is to make the monologue an address to someone specific. I have a friend I've tried to convince to buy a specific ketchup, car, credit card, and so on. Of course, he doesn't know this because I'm not talking to him when I'm trying to convince him of how great these products are. Rather, I'm talking to a camera, but I'm imagining that I'm talking to him. This changes my aspect from "salesperson trying to sell you something" to "concerned friend trying to help you out." In a similar way, radio announcers are taught to imagine that they are talking to just one person over the air.

The same idea can be used in your proclamation. If you're proclaiming to your whole community in general, then your proclamation is likely to have a general feel to it. But if you imagine yourself speaking to one person in particular, your proclamation will seem more like genuine communication and will be easier for the community to connect to. You're less likely to proclaim in a formal, preachy way which distances the community and makes the reading difficult to understand.

When you choose a person to speak to, make it a very specific person. Don't just make it "a friend," but rather make it a specific friend with a name and a face, preferably someone you speak to at least occasionally. Really try to imagine that person sitting before you as you proclaim. In your proclamation, you'll still want to make eye contact with everyone in the community. If you find it difficult to keep this person in mind as you proclaim to the entire community, then at least use the technique when you practice.

You don't always have to choose the same person. In fact, try to specify someone who needs to hear the intention you are proclaiming. You may use different people for different readings, but it's probably best not to specify someone who will be in the congregation when you proclaim. Having your chosen recipient actually there may be distracting, and you may be tempted to continually check in to see this person's response during your reading.

Many lectors I've worked with have been surprised by how powerful specificity is and how profoundly it transforms their proclamation. Try it once or twice yourself and I think you'll see what I mean.

Community Context

This brings up another context we must consider when discerning our intention. In addition to the scriptural, liturgical, and lectionary contexts, we must also consider the community context. We must be aware of what is going on in the community when we proclaim. There are two places to read this context.

First, the context may be defined for you if your community is focusing on something specific for the day, season, or year. The liturgy committee may have asked the liturgical ministers to focus on the "in-between-ness" of the season of Advent this year, or on the call for social justice during this Lent. This may be a day of remembrance for the community or an anniversary celebration. This year may be designated a special year of reconciliation by your community or by the larger community of the universal Church. We often think that such ideas apply only to the music ministry or the homilists, but we need to be aware of them in our ministry of the Word as well. If they exist, even for the single day's celebration, we need to consider them as we consider the intent of our reading, though we may not always be able to use them.

The second place to read the context of the community is in the community's (and your own) experience. What has been going on in the community recently? Have there been some sorrows or joys? You are going to proclaim "Rejoice in the Lord always!" slightly differently to a community struggling with unemployment than to one welcoming home a mission group.

If your own community is beset by divisions, you may choose the unity intention for the earlier example. If your community is struggling with prejudice, you may choose the challenge to stop judging. Consider also what is happening in the larger community outside your church walls. What message needs to be heard by your city, state, or nation?

The strongest and best intentions are ones that move the community to *respond*. It's the ultimate intention of all Scripture to move its hearers to a response. Scripture is not just a collection of nice stories for our entertainment, though that's not to say that they can't be entertaining. But their purpose is to effect change. "When God communicates his word, he expects a response."[6] As James reminds us, "Be doers of the word and not hearers only" (1:22).

Thus, when choosing an intention, try not to tell the community something they already know; tell them what they need to know, or even better, something they need to do. Instead of "I want to teach them about the origins of Passover," try, "I want them to rely on God to release them from slavery." "Be free!" is the command.

Phrasing an intention this way gives us as proclaimers an *action* to play. Action is what brings energy, tension, and, yes, drama to a proclamation, a play, and real life. Think: Aren't the most exciting times in our lives when we are *going for something*, when we have drive and desire, and, most especially, when we have obstacles to overcome? That's why watching sports is exciting. That's why movies are made about people who succeed against incredible odds: lovers who become separated but find each other again, the man who survives all alone on a desert island, the rebel forces who bring down an evil empire. In this sense, all movies are action movies.

When we read with an action in mind, we also connect more strongly with the community. All of a sudden, eye contact is not just a thing we do because we were *taught* to do it; it becomes something we do because we *need* to do it to get our community to change. Our voice naturally takes on more inflection; we speak with more passion; we work to connect because we need to get our community to respond to this message.

Now, let's take a look at an exhortatory passage:

> The LORD addressed Job out of the storm and said:
>> Who shut within doors the sea,
>>> when it burst forth from the womb;
>> when I made the clouds its garment
>>> and thick darkness its swaddling bands?
>> When I set limits for it
>> and fastened the bar of its door,

6. Introduction, *Lectionary for Mass*, 6.

and said: Thus far shall you come but no farther,

and here shall your proud waves be stilled!

(Job 38:1, 8–11; Ordinary 12B[7])

First, we need to consider the point of view from which this passage is written. It's obvious in the earlier passage from Romans that, since Paul was the author, we were looking for Paul's intention. In this passage, however, the author of Job put these words into God's mouth, so we need to discern God's intention as a character in this drama. Looking at the scriptural context of chapter 38 and the accompanying commentaries, we learn that this is the beginning of God's response to Job's questioning. The overall theme of this response is, basically, "Who are you to question my actions?" Within the context of the other readings for the day (the Gospel is Mark 4:35–41, Jesus calming the storm), the theme might be expressed as "I have control over the sea and all elements."

But if we want to find an intention that requires a response (from Job as well as our community), we might express the intention as "God wants Job to acknowledge God's power over the sea." Remember, before we use the intention in our proclamation, we direct it from ourselves toward the community. So the intention becomes "I want you to acknowledge God's power over the sea." Now, unless you have a large seafaring community, you might want to personalize this even more and make your intention, "I want you to acknowledge God's power over your lives." Or more directly, "Acknowledge God's power over your lives."

You may find yourself uncomfortable speaking the words of God, especially when you personalize the intention in this way. But notice that even though you make God's desire your own, you're not asking the community to acknowledge *your* power but God's. When we speak the words of God in this way, we're continuing in the tradition of the prophets.

Notice that discovering an intention hasn't required us to change one word of Scripture; rather, the intention has come directly from these words. Sometimes, in fact, an intention is right there in the reading: Seek the Lord! (Isaiah 55:6–9; Ordinary 25A). Be glad and exult! (Zephaniah 3:14–18a; Advent 3C). Avoid immorality! (1 Corinthians 6:13c–15a; 17–20; Ordinary 2B[8]). This is especially true in exhortatory texts.

If, however, after much prayer and discernment and reading of contexts, you're still having trouble finding an intention, see if one of these fits:

❖ *I want you to acknowledge that God loves you!* "A love note from God" was how I once heard Scripture described. "God loves you" summarizes the intention of all Scripture. There are some tough passages in the Old Testament describing the wrath of God or the destruction of Israel's enemies. If you're having trouble finding an intention for those passages, try this one. They are examples of how much God loves God's own.

7. Proper 7B.
8. Epiphany 2B.

✤ *I want you to repent and believe the good news!* This is the message Jesus came to proclaim (Mark 1:15). We find this intention in much of the Gospels and the epistles. Sometimes the first part of the intention (Repent!) is all that's there, especially in some readings from the Old Testament. These are often not the most comfortable readings to hear.

✤ *I want you to love God and love your neighbor as yourself!* Jesus said that this was the intention behind "the whole law and the prophets" (Matthew 22:40). Again, some readings focus on the first part, some on the second.

Intention makes our reading come alive and directs it toward the community. It gives urgency to our proclamation; it makes concrete our desire to communicate to the community. Intention returns the *need to communicate* to our ministry, and once this need is there, reading really starts to become proclamation.

Multiple Intentions

Let's look at another passage, this time a narrative text (Luke 9:18–24; Ordinary 12C):

> Once when Jesus was praying in solitude,
>> and the disciples were with him,
>> he asked them, "Who do the crowds say that I am?"
> They said in reply, "John the Baptist;
>> others, Elijah;
>> still others, 'One of the ancient prophets has arisen.'"
> Then he said to them, "But who do you say that I am?"
> Peter said in reply, "The Christ of God."
> He rebuked them
>> and directed them not to tell this to anyone.
>
> He said, "The Son of Man must suffer greatly
>> and be rejected by the elders, the chief priests, and the scribes,
>> and be killed and on the third day be raised."
> Then he said to all,
>> "If anyone wishes to come after me, he must deny himself
>> and take up his cross daily and follow me.
> For whoever wishes to save his life will lose it,
>> but whoever loses his life for my sake will save it."

First, let's look at the points of view in this passage. The overall point of view is Luke's. What is his intention in this passage? Why, out of all the stories that were available to him, did he choose to include this one (which is to say, why did the storytellers of the early Christian community decide to keep telling this story)? One possibility is to show Peter as the one among the disciples who acknowledges Jesus as the Christ. Indeed, commentaries point out that Luke has left out Peter's refusal to accept Jesus as a suffering Messiah, which occurs in Mark's account of this incident. But Luke is not writing a mere history lesson. Remembering that his intention is directed toward his readers, it might be better expressed as "Luke wants his readers to acknowledge Jesus as Christ." There are other possibilities. The complementary first reading for the day (Zechariah 12:10–11; 13:1) points up Jesus' assertion that, though he is Christ, he will suffer greatly. In the last part of Luke's passage, Jesus emphasizes that his followers, too, will suffer. Thus the intention could also be "Luke wants his readers to know they will suffer just as Christ did." But a shorter and even better intention is found in the reading itself: "Deny yourself!"

In fact, in this reading, as is the case in some longer readings, we might decide that Luke has two intentions: In the first part, the intention is "Acknowledge Jesus as your Christ!" In the last part, the intention is "Deny yourself!" There's nothing wrong with finding multiple intentions in a text. In general, a dramatic text will have one main intention, sometimes called the *spine* of the text. For example, each of the Gospels has an overall intention based on the circumstances of the writer and his audience. But within each Gospel, the writer has specific intentions for each part of the Gospel story that he relates. These intentions support their overall intention. Although it's helpful to know the writer's overall intention, we need to uncover the specific intentions related to the excerpt that we proclaim.

Think of athletes whose intention it is to compete in the Olympics. Although this is their overall intention, they need to break it down into specific actions, each of which also has an intention. When they work with weights, although their overall intention is still to compete in the Olympics, their specific intention is to build muscle mass. When they go running, their specific intention is to build endurance. When they work with their coach, their specific intention is to improve technique. All these intentions support their overall intention of getting to the Olympics.

You see, of course, that this can lead to an infinite regression of intentions, until we are trying to find an intention for each word of Scripture. Some actors do exactly that with their scripts. In addition to an overall intention for their part in the piece, they try to find a specific intention for each scene, and then for each line of dialogue in those scenes (like the actor in the joke at the beginning of this chapter). Likewise, in the world of Scripture scholarship, very long dissertations have been written on why an author chose one particular word. Attention to such minutia may be less productive for us as lectors.

There is one place where it is helpful to discern multiple intentions, however, and that's in narrative texts with multiple characters. Characters in a narrative text each have their own point of view and therefore their own intention. Thus, in the above text, we can identify an intention for Jesus, Peter, and the other disciples (who are treated as a whole here). The obvious intention in Jesus' question is: "I want to know who people say that I am." He might also have another intention: "I want to give the disciples a chance to acknowledge me as Christ. I want the disciples to deny themselves as I deny myself." The other disciples might have this intention: "We want the Lord to tell us who he is because we're unsure ourselves." Peter's intention might be, as it often is, "I want to show the Lord I acknowledge him as my Savior (and I'm willing to follow him without reservation)." Of course, Peter often fails in his execution of this intention, and that's all right. An intention doesn't have to be successful. Look at the prophets. How often did their intentions fail? In every story, some characters fail to achieve their intentions. This is what gives a story conflict and sustains our interest. Some people win, some people lose.

Just because we know that a character will fail to achieve their intention in the end, we shouldn't create an intention to fail. This is another example of telegraphing, playing the end at the beginning, and it's a dangerous trap for actors and proclaimers.

Sometimes an intention may not agree with what a character says or does. This happens in our own life a lot. We may say something that completely contradicts what we really mean, like our put-upon teenager of a few chapters ago who said, "I'll be happy to take out the garbage." The following narrative is an example:

> After the man, Adam, had eaten of the tree,
>> the Lord GOD called to the man and asked him, "Where are you?"
> He answered, "I heard you in the garden;
>> but I was afraid, because I was naked,
>> so I hid myself."
> Then he asked,
>> "Who told you that you were naked?
> You have eaten, then,
>> from the tree of which I had forbidden you to eat!"
> The man replied, "The woman whom you put here with me—
>> she gave me fruit from the tree, and so I ate it."
> The LORD God then asked the woman,
> "Why did you do such a thing?"
> The woman answered,
>> "The serpent tricked me into it, so I ate it."
>
> (Genesis 3:9–15; Ordinary 10B[9])

On the surface, God's questioning implies that God's intention is "I want to find out what happened." But God already knows what happened, so here is an intention that conflicts with what is being said. What might God's intention be? The tone of this entire proclamation hinges on our choice. Having God's intention as "I want to toy with Adam and Eve for disobeying me" makes for a very different reading from "I want to give Adam and Eve a chance to be honest." See if you can find intentions for Adam and Eve in this reading, and remember that intentions and words don't always agree.

---

9. Proper 5B.

When you identify the intention for a reading, write it down—in big, bold letters—at the top of your text, so you're reminded of it every time you practice the reading. In a narrative text or one with multiple intentions, write the intention in the margin whenever it changes for the reading or for a character. You won't proclaim using your rehearsal copy, but you'll come to associate these intentions with the reading through your practice.

Using Intention

You see now, I hope, how intention is really at the core of your proclamation and pulls all the other elements together. Tempo, inflection, rhythm, volume, eye contact, posture, and emotion (which I'll discuss next) will all be affected by your intention. Although you'll still need to be conscious of these technical details, your intention will guide you in how to use them. The stronger your intention and the more central to your proclamation you make it, the less you'll need to adjust these elements. They'll adjust themselves if you really make the intention your own.

And if you've identified some choice words in your text, here's where the choice comes in. Your intention will determine the choice you make about these words when you proclaim them. That's why it's impossible to say whether choice words are to be stressed or unstressed or how they're to be inflected. Your intention will guide the choices you make about these words.

If you're having trouble with your intention and if all these other elements are not falling into place, then you may have chosen an intention that is not really supported by the text. You may be trying to force something on the text that isn't really there. In this case, you should look again at the text, the contexts, and ask again for the wisdom of the Spirit to identify a different intention.

Never approach the ambo without an intention, thinking that all you're about to do is proclaim. Let me repeat that. Never approach the ambo thinking that what you're about to do is proclaim! What you're about to do is *change the community so radically that they conform themselves completely to Christ, who* is, after all, the Word you proclaim. Next time you're asked why you read, this is your answer. This is your overall intention as a lector; this is the spine of your whole ministry; this is your Olympics. Each specific intention you choose for an individual proclamation must support this spine. As you approach the ambo, repeat your intention silently to yourself a couple of times. "Be hopeful!" "Acknowledge the power of God!" "Deny yourselves!" In acting terms, we say, "Play your intention, not your words! Focus on your action, not your lines!"

As you do this, you may realize that you have no control over whether or not the community changes. And you are correct; the change is up to them. But that should not stop you from proclaiming. Did Hosea stop prophesying when Israel continued to be faithless? Did knowing that he had no control over the behavior of the Philippians stop Paul from telling them to rejoice in the Lord? For your community, you are Hosea, you are Paul, you are Luke, and you are

Christ! You are there not only to proclaim the words of these people, you are there to proclaim their intentions.

And if you don't, who will?

> I then heard the voice of the Lord saying: "Whom shall I send? Who will go for us?" And I said, "Here am I, send me!" (Isaiah 6:8 NJB)

Four Important Things to Remember about Intention

1. Choose an intention to give yourself a need to communicate. A reading may have multiple intentions. For a narrative text, choose an intention for each character.

2. An intention answers the question "What is the author trying to say? What is the central point of this message?" To discern intention, take the text into prayer and read the commentaries and the contexts (including the community context).

3. Personalize the intention so it is directed from *you* to *your community:* "I want you to _____." The strongest intentions are those that require a response from the community.

4. Your goal as a proclaimer is to change the community so they conform themselves completely to Christ!

Chapter 6

Working on Emotion: We're All Brothers and Sisters under the Skin

I once heard a fellow actor complain about the constant barrage of well-meaning people who tell us that we shouldn't feel bad when we don't get a part or when we get a critical review. "Of course we're going to feel bad," he said. "That's what we do for a living. We get paid to feel." It's true. Actors are professional feelers, so to speak.

And that's a very important job in any culture. We have a communal need to express emotion. When tragedy happens, sometimes it's only the artists—actors, storytellers, musicians—who can really express the feelings of a community. We look to them for that. We know it's unhealthy to keep feelings bottled up inside, unexpressed. But when they are too painful or difficult to express, we look outside ourselves to these artists for emotional release. And not just for challenging feelings like sorrow, remorse, and forgiveness. Feelings like joy and peace and love can be just as difficult for us to express, especially when we don't really feel them. Look at all the feelings expressed by David and the other writers of the psalms. They expressed not only their own feelings but also the feelings of an entire nation. The lector-storyteller fulfills a similarly valuable and necessary role on behalf of the community.

The characters of Scripture were highly emotional: Moses showed his fear in encountering God and his anger at the Israelites' faithlessness. The emotions of the prophets still ring in their words today. And, of course, Jesus showed his emotion very freely in public: He wept over the death of Lazarus, got angry over the moneychangers in the temple, and cursed the duplicity of the self-righteous religious leaders. I imagine those who first stood up to tell their eyewitness stories about Jesus did so with great emotion.

Emotion is a key element for turning a reading into a proclamation. It's also the element most feared by lectors. This is to be expected. We are not used to—and are even discouraged from—showing our emotions in public, especially in church. But, once again, since we have committed to telling the *whole* story of Scripture with all our verbal and nonverbal skills, we must proclaim emotion as well.

Remember Walter Wangerin's instructions to the Christmas storyteller? "When you speak of *loving*, seem to *love*. Describing *sorrow*, be *sad*. Let *fear* come through a *harried* voice, and *gladness* come with *laughter*, and *triumph* sound like *exultation*." The work of the storyteller, as Wangerin describes it, is all about emotion: "It is you who will *love* or not, and so the story will or will not *love*" (emphasis mine).[1]

Emotion is one of the primary nonverbal communicators. We respond to emotion very quickly, even before we know what's going to be said. If I were to approach you with a concerned look and say, slowly, in a low tone and with sadness in my voice, "I have some news for you," you'd likely be very worried about what I was about to say. But if I were to run up to you excitedly, with eyes shining, energy in my voice, and quickly say, "I have some news for you," you'd probably be eager to hear the news. Notice that the words are exactly the same in both situations, yet the meaning is completely different. The difference is conveyed entirely through emotion. Thus when we fail to proclaim with emotion, we make the reading more difficult for our community to understand.

Intention alone is not enough. An intention tells us *what* we want to say; emotion tells us *how* we say it. Emotion is the energy that fuels the drive of our intention. One armchair psychologist definition of "e-motion" is "energy in motion," and, in fact, emotion is what gives our intentions drive.

A single intention can be driven by different emotions in different people or circumstances. If my intention is to get you to be hopeful, I can be stern, cajoling, joyful, humorous—even anxious—as I act on my intention. Some of these emotions may fit my task better than others, so I need to choose carefully. And like intention, my choice must be supported by the text.

Making an Emotional Choice

Some choices are plainly evident in the text. If it says Paul is rejoicing, or Jeremiah is grumbling, or God is acting with compassion, then the emotion we need to express is clear. In most cases, though, we must make our own choice. Intention is a good starting point. (Some actors will connect first with the emotion of a text and then find the intention. You may work this way as well, if you find it more useful.)

Sometimes the intention we choose is so direct that our emotional energy follows naturally as we proclaim with the intention in mind. This is often the case if we have a personal connection to the intention. For example, if the intention we choose for our proclamation is, "Stop judging each other," and we have recently had an experience of judging or being judged, our emotional expression may come without our really identifying it first. But this is not always the case, especially when we are not used to expressing emotion in our reading. In these cases, we need to work specifically on identifying the emotional content of the text and bringing it to our proclamation.

Let's look again at the text from Romans:

> Brothers and sisters:
>
> None of us lives for oneself, and no one dies for oneself.

---

1. "The Christmas Story," in *The Manger Is Empty: Stories in Time* (San Francisco: Harper and Row, 1989), 27.

> For if we live, we live for the Lord,
>
>> and if we die, we die for the Lord;
>
>> so then, whether we live or die, we are the Lord's.
>
> For this is why Christ died and came to life,
>
>> that he might be Lord of both the dead and the living.
>
> (Romans 14:7–9; Ordinary 24A[2])

First, look at the intention. If we choose the intention "Stop judging each other," then Paul's emotion might be *anger* or *frustration*. Similar emotions may flow from the intention "End your divisions and be unified." But these emotions aren't really justified when we choose the intention "I want you to hope." For this intention, we need to choose a complementary emotion.

A challenge with didactic texts such as this is that they often seem emotionless; after all, their purpose is to teach. (In fact, strong emotion within a didactic text would qualify it as exhortatory.) But emotion is certainly there.

Consider the emotional relationship between teachers and their students, or, better yet, between pastors and their flocks. There is a whole range of emotions in such a relationship. Teachers express their satisfaction with the progress of their students or their annoyance at their stubbornness. In their relationship with their community, pastors can feel angry, caring, grim, fiery, playful, smug—I'm sure you can add a few of your own!

When no specific emotion seems present in a didactic text, the emotion that's there is *love*. A teaching is given out of love for the community, in a desire for the community to grow in its relationship with God and with each other. As you proclaim a didactic text, do so out of your own love for the community.

Now let's turn to the exhortatory passage from Job:

> The LORD addressed Job out of the storm and said:
>
> Who shut within doors the sea,
>
>> when it burst forth from the womb;
>
> when I made the clouds its garment
>
>> and thick darkness its swaddling bands?
>
> When I set limits for it
>
>> and fastened the bar of its door,
>
> and said: Thus far shall you come but no farther,
>
>> and here shall your proud waves be stilled!
>
> (Job 38:1,8–11; Ordinary 12B[3])

In the last chapter, we decided on the intention "I want you to acknowledge God as all-powerful in your lives." What might be the emotional energy driving that intention? First of all, God is addressing Job out of a storm. This is not a quiet sort of teaching out of concern for Job! God wants to make a point

---

2. Proper 19A.

3. Proper 7B.

emphatically; the storm is the exclamation point. That's why this is an exhortatory text, and why the emotion we choose must be heightened.

A few possibilities that come to mind immediately are *frustrated, angry,* even *boastful* or *proud.* God might be *annoyed* by Job as we would be annoyed by a gnat that buzzes around our eyes. There's a sense of irony in these lines, so God could even be *amused* by Job as he mocks him with these rhetorical questions. Any of these possibilities could be supported by the text and the intention. Again, the choice is ours, part of our responsibility as proclaimer.

Just as it seemed strange to find an intention for God, it may also seem strange to find emotion for God. Yet Scripture is full of God's emotion. Our emotions, in fact, are an image of God's own emotions. Emotions are neither good nor bad, although the action that springs from them may be. There's nothing wrong with expressing these negative emotions. We wouldn't get very far in the Bible if everyone had only warm and fuzzy emotions. There's nothing wrong with the "lighter" emotions in church either, like amusement or irony. If you don't think God has a sense of humor, just look at a platypus! (Also see "Funny How?" below.)

Funny How?

Stories wouldn't get very far without humor. Every good storyteller knows that humor is essential, even (especially) in the most dramatic stories. The good storytellers who conveyed to us the stories that became our Scripture must have known this, too, because there is much humor in these stories. They've been layered over with so many centuries of gilding and lacquer that the humor may be hard to find, but if we miss it, the story loses a great deal of its value.

Humor is not only jokes, although there are many jokes in Scripture. Humor is an attitude. It's what keeps us sane in a world that seems insane at times. It's the ability to look at a grim situation and still laugh. It's realizing that nothing makes sense and finding that funny. In this way, humor is a gift of faith. It's our ability to say, with Job, "Well, things are really, really bad right now, but I think I'll still trust in God, even though that makes no sense at all." Now *that's* funny!

Our work of proclaiming is serious, but it's not deadly serious. We need to keep a sense of humor about what we do. This will help us find the humor in Scripture. Paraphrasing is a great way to see the humor in a text. When you free yourself from the formal words, you may find the irony, wit, or absurdity inherent in the story, however serious it is.

We have a few examples of humorous texts in this chapter, or at least a few examples of texts that can be given a humorous interpretation if we choose. God's response to Job could be tinged with a wry annoyance: "And, excuse me, but exactly who are you? Did I see you around when I created the seas? When was the last time you quieted a storm?" The story of Adam and Eve has a lot of humor as well: "It wasn't our fault! It was that *woman*—it was that *snake*—that *you* put here! We're innocent!"

Here are a few other examples. You can find many others on your own:

- In the story of the man born blind, the man responds to the questioning of the authorities by saying, "Why do you want to hear [about Jesus] again? Do you want to become his disciples, too?" (John 9:27b). Oh, sure they do!

- Abraham's persistence in his argument with God over the destruction of Sodom and Gomorrah has much humor in it (Genesis

18:20–32). Look, for example, at how Abraham abases himself each time he addresses God; he is obsequious to the point of being silly.

✤ When some in the crowd accuse the disciples of being drunk on Pentecost, Peter responds: "What, do you think we're drunk? It's only nine o'clock in the morning" (Acts 2:15 paraphrased).

Now, we don't need to proclaim these passages as though they were a stand-up routine. Most comedy is played seriously. We laugh because we recognize the humor, but many times the characters themselves don't know they're being funny. That's not to say that if you recognize the humor in a story, you can't let the community in on the joke. While I wouldn't recommend going so far as to wink at them, you can indicate in your voice and demeanor that this might be funny. Your community may not feel comfortable laughing or even smiling, but at least you can give them permission to do so if they choose.

If you're stuck choosing an emotion for your reading, the table on page 83 may help. Emotions can be divided into four basic groups: happiness, sadness, anger, and fear—otherwise known as *glad*, *sad*, *mad*, and *scared*. (Some might add a few more categories such as love, which is really part of *glad*; *shame* or *hurt*, which are part of *sad*; or *frustration*, which is part of *angry*). I've provided a list of varying emotions in these categories; I'm sure you will be able to find the emotions expressed in your reading in this list, even if you have to go through the list word by word until you find the emotion that fits. The list also shows the broad variance of emotions that we can express. Instead of being angry, I could be *belligerent* or *testy* or *bitter* or *outraged*. I culled this list from more than five hundred emotions; I suspect there are at least that many more.

Changing Emotions

We've already seen that in a narrative text with multiple characters, each of those characters will have their own intentions in addition to the overall intention of the writer. Likewise, in such a text, each of the characters will also have their own emotions in addition to the overall emotion of the writer.

Here is our narrative text from Luke from the last chapter:

> Once when Jesus was praying in solitude,
>> and the disciples were with him,
>> he asked them, "Who do the crowds say that I am?"
> They said in reply, "John the Baptist;
>> others, Elijah;
>> still others, 'One of the ancient prophets has arisen.'"
> Then he said to them, "But who do you say that I am?"
> Peter said in reply, "The Christ of God."
> He rebuked them
>> and directed them not to tell this to anyone.

He said, "The Son of Man must suffer greatly

> and be rejected by the elders, the chief priests, and the scribes,

> and be killed and on the third day be raised."

Then he said to all,

> "If anyone wishes to come after me, he must deny himself

> and take up his cross daily and follow me.

For whoever wishes to save his life will lose it,

> but whoever loses his life for my sake will save it."

> (Luke 9:18–24; Ordinary 12C)

Look at the emotional cues in the text. Jesus is found praying in solitude. Perhaps he is *contemplative*, *peaceful*, or *secure*. The disciples might be *anxious*, *eager*, or *confused* as they answer his question. Peter might be *confident* or even *arrogant* as he answers Jesus. But then Jesus rebukes them. This implies a sharp censure. He might be *angry*, but more likely he is *firm* or *brusque*. As he prophesies his own death, there are any number of emotions we could choose: *sad*, *triumphant*, *cautious*, *anxious*. Then he moves to the message: "Deny yourself." Again, he may be *firm* or even *joyful*, as he reveals the key to saving one's life

Lines of narration in a text like this deserve special mention. There are two ways to read the lines written from the narrator's point of view. One is to read them with the intention and emotion of the author. The other is to read the lines about a character with the intention and emotion of that character. For example, when you read, "He rebuked them," read it with the emotion of Jesus' rebuke, and the line will have more power.

A text doesn't need to have multiple characters to have multiple emotions. It doesn't even need to have multiple intentions.

A text with a single intention can have multiple emotions behind it. It's the same in our lives. My intention to finish a big project at work may first be fueled by my pride in being asked to do it. Then pleasure from doing something I enjoy may sustain my action, but as the deadline approaches, fear may take over. All these emotions drive a single intention.

Look at this text from Paul's Second Letter to Timothy. It is a narrative, as it tells the story of Paul's past and his expectations for the future.

> Beloved:

> I am already being poured out like a libation,

> > and the time of my departure is at hand.

> I have competed well; I have finished the race;

> > I have kept the faith.

> From now on the crown of righteousness awaits me,

> > which the Lord, the just judge,

> > will award to me on that day, and not only to me,

> > but to all who have longed for his appearance.

One Hundred Seventy-Five Emotion Words

Glad

euphoric	fearless	up	joyful	thoughtful	grateful
peaceful	energetic	celebratory	serene	pleased	happy
victorious	confident	exultant	self-righteous	agreeable	delighted
playful	courageous	affectionate	conceited	loving	rejoicing
funny	reflective	composed	proud	passionate	humorous
boastful	overjoyed	collected	contemplative	calm	cool
hopeful	secure	tender	smug	satisfied	cheerful
tongue-in-cheek	relaxed	lighthearted	warm	encouraged	content
jovial	self-assured	jubilant	mellow	quiet	moderate
festive	pensive	pleasant	gentle	enthusiastic	excited
zealous					

Sad

ashamed	regretful	unhappy	guilty	desolate	lonely
anguished	grieving	disappointed	apologetic	low	sorrowful
despondent	somber	tired	troubled	penitent	dejected
weary	suffering	contrite	pained	serious	cynical
repentant	pessimistic	discouraged	vain	distressed	glum
hopeless	hurting	worthless	weepy	sorry	miserable
grim	despairing	solemn	bored	down	depressed
bereaved	mournful	afflicted	helpless	bad	

Mad

irritated	critical	annoyed	hateful	testy	offended
enraged	stormy	combative	vexed	acerbic	cranky
cruel	hostile	evil	mean	irate	angry
gruff	fiery	violent	belligerent	grumpy	irked
exasperated	disagreeable	sardonic	upset	sarcastic	furious

Scared

alarmed	reluctant	nervous	frustrated	petrified	afraid
panicked	uneasy	horrified	amazed	apprehensive	worried
distraught	confused	restless	cowardly	stunned	overwhelmed
anxious	cautious	timid	awestruck	surprised	bothered
shy	indecisive	frightened	fearful	terrified	shocked
concerned	uncertain	humble			

At my first defense no one appeared on my behalf,

    but everyone deserted me.

May it not be held against them!

But the Lord stood by me and gave me strength,

    so that through me the proclamation might be completed

    and all the Gentiles might hear it.

And I was rescued from the lion's mouth.

The Lord will rescue me from every evil threat

    and will bring me safe to his heavenly kingdom.

To him be glory forever and ever. Amen.

2 Timothy 4:6–8, 16–18; Ordinary 30C[4]

First, see if you can isolate an intention. Why is Paul telling this story? Perhaps Paul is encouraging Timothy to persevere and finish the race as well. We can phrase this intention for our community as "I want you to persevere and finish the race."

Now let's take a closer look at all the emotions that come up for Paul as he recounts this story in support of this intention. First, looking into the background for the text, we find that Paul is at the end of his life, writing this from prison (2 Timothy 1:8). There is some question about whether this letter was actually written by Paul. If it wasn't, then the writer added these very personal statements to give weight to the claim of Pauline authorship. In this case, this excerpt reads much like a biographical play, in which a playwright creates a fictional account of a real person's life. Whoever the author, the text is emotionally strong.

How might Paul feel at this time? Look at the expression *poured out*. It refers to the action of pouring out a cup of wine onto a sacrifice or onto a grave. It's a very rich image. Paul might be satisfied that his life is an offering for Christ, but he might also be very tired. Move from this emotion to its stronger cousin: *exhaustion*. A stronger choice is a better choice if it can be supported by the text. Paul certainly has every right to be exhausted at this point in his life!

Then Paul shifts: "I have competed well." This doesn't sound like he's tired anymore; more like he's *satisfied* and *confident*. Skip down to "At my first defense, no one appeared on my behalf, but everyone deserted me. May it not be held against them." Even though he is forgiving, his words sound tinged with a little *anger* as well. Remember, don't shy away from these "negative" emotions. Paul is a human being; allow him to be angry. He has a right to this emotion as well.

See if you can find other emotions in the text. As you do, draw a line between the changes in emotion on your practice copy and write the emotions in the margin.

On the next page, I've scored the text with one possible flow of emotions; other combinations are defensible as well.

---

4. Proper 25C.

loving	Beloved:
exhausted	I am already being poured out like a libation, and the time of my departure is at hand.
satisfied	I have competed well; I have finished the race; I have kept the faith.

joyful	From now on the crown of righteousness awaits me,
	     which the Lord, the just judge,
	     will award to me on that day, and not only to me,
	     but to all who have longed for his appearance.

angry	At my first defense no one appeared on my behalf, but everyone deserted me. May it not be held against them!
peaceful	But the Lord stood by me and gave me strength, so that through me the proclamation might be completed and all the Gentiles might hear it. And I was rescued from the lion's mouth.
confident	The Lord will rescue me from every evil threat and will bring me safe to his heavenly kingdom.
exultant	To him be glory forever and ever. Amen.

It may seem strange or difficult to change emotions very quickly when you proclaim a narrative text like this, but our emotions turn on a dime all the time: We get a good grade on the exam we thought we had flunked; our team comes from behind with a stunning play; someone we love pays us a surprise visit. We don't transition slowly from emotion to emotion; we switch immediately with each new stimulus.

Listen to a piece of music, especially a classical or jazz piece. Listen to how the emotional rhythm changes. Even some hymns change emotion from refrain to verse or from verse to verse. A short piece may have few changes, but a longer piece may have many emotions. This change is what keeps the music (and similarly our proclamations) interesting and keeps the community tuned in. It also helps the community understand the text as the emotions set off the various thoughts of the text. To help you proclaim these quick changes, work with the exercise on changing emotions in "Tuning Your Piano" (page 86).

Expressing Emotion

Now you've looked at the text and decided which emotions are appropriate. How do you bring that emotion to your reading? You can't just write down "joyful" and expect to turn it on when you read!

As I said earlier, sometimes our emotional expression will come in our proclamation without really having to identify it, especially if the intention is strong or close to something in our own lives. Also, if we're using the technique of *specificity*, described in the last chapter, then our emotional response may come easily when we imagine ourselves directing our intention toward a specific person.

We need to be careful, however, that our emotional response is justified by the text. If we happen to be angry as we proclaim, or if we're angry with the

Tuning Your Piano

Actors need to have all their emotions available at all times. Emotions are like keys of a piano. If I'm playing a concerto and strike a certain key, I expect it to make a sound. If it doesn't, the whole concerto falls apart. But when it comes to the keys of our emotions, we may find that some keys don't work. Conditioning from our parents, our friends, and our culture has taught us that we are not allowed to express some emotions: "Boys don't cry." "Christians don't get angry." "Pride goes before a fall." We already noted how difficult some of the "negative" emotions are for us to express, especially in church. But when we're called upon to express these emotions in our reading, we need to be able to access them. When we reach for a key, we need it to sound every time.

I'm not suggesting that every lector needs to find a psychotherapist. But I am suggesting that we need to be aware of our conditioning about emotion and of what emotions we find difficult to express. When you have time, go through the list of emotions on page 83 and try to identify the ones you are most and least comfortable with. A good exercise is to try to recall the last time you expressed each of these emotions: What were the circumstances? How did you express the emotion? What happened in your voice, body, and mind when you felt this way?

As you go through the list, you may find it difficult to even know what your emotions are. This is not uncommon. Practice becoming aware of your emotions. Every so often, take out this list and try to identify how you're feeling. Slowly, you'll become more aware of your feelings and also more aware of how you express those feelings. Then, when you're called on to express emotion in a proclamation, you'll know what should be happening.

Here's an exercise to work on conveying emotion quickly, on really tuning your piano. This exercise works best if you have someone work with you. First, choose something to read aloud; if you can, use a narrative text, like a story or novel, but anything, even part of this book, will do. Ask your friend to call out a random emotion during the reading, using the list in this chapter as a guide. Begin reading in a neutral tone. As soon as your friend calls out an emotion, immediately begin to read with that emotion. Your friend should allow you to read with this emotion for a few moments, and then call out another emotion, which you must immediately start expressing. Continue this exercise until you've practiced with a number of emotions. It doesn't matter if the emotions fit with what you're reading; in fact, the exercise works better if they don't. The key is to learn to access emotions quickly. You will also become more comfortable expressing these emotions in front of someone else.

If you have no one to work with you, select the emotions beforehand, and mark certain points in the text where you will switch. Even better, write a number of emotions down on slips of paper and put them in a pile; then at the points you want to switch, grab a slip of paper and immediately switch to that emotion.

person we've chosen as our specific listener, then we will bring that anger to the reading whether or not it's appropriate. (You might have a hard time justifying anger as the emotion behind a proclamation like "Rejoice, O daughter Jerusalem!") For these reasons, even if the intention or our work with specificity brings up an emotional response, we need to check it against the text.

And what if we find that the response is not justified? Or what if we are able to get no response at all? Then we need to do some emotional work, and here's where the fun begins!

Emotions are slippery fellows. If I'm directing a scene and one of my actors is not bringing the emotion I want to the scene, I know I have to approach the subject delicately. To simply say, "I think you need to be more frightened by him," is likely to bring about wide eyes, fluttering hands, a stammering voice, and all sorts of other big and obvious signs of "fright," none of which will be believable. This is especially the case with beginning actors, who have yet to learn how to translate such requests from directors into something they can work with.

To name an emotional problem is to bring the pink elephant into the room. As soon as the emotion is named, the actor can think of nothing else, and, of course, *thinking* of it squelches all possibility of *experiencing* it. This is such a challenge for actors that more time is spent on it in acting classes and more ink is spent on it in acting books than on any other subject. But lucky for us, all that effort has produced a few helpful ideas.

Get It from the Story

It's worth emphasizing again that the best source of emotion is the story you proclaim. I always find it easier to play a big emotional scene in a play when it occurs late in the script (as it usually does, thankfully), because I've had the preceding hour or so to inhabit the character and his intentions. Any heightened emotions come more naturally out of the lived experience of the play. But sometimes an actor is called upon to enter a scene with a strong emotion without the benefit of a few scenes' worth of buildup.

And in movies, scenes are rarely even filmed in the order they appear in the script. An actor may be required to react emotionally to something that happened moments ago in the story but was filmed days ago or may be filmed a week hence.

In these cases, we may not be able to get the emotion from the story, so we need to move to the next technique.

Imagination

Imagination is an actor's stock-in-trade. Whenever I act, I'm required to imagine myself as someone I'm not: a Danish prince, a soldier in World War I, a famous composer, an Irish barkeeper. One of the things that make acting so seductive is that actors get to *play* all the time. Imagination is the mind at play. It's a talent we're all born with; it's a gift from being made in the image of God. And yet, as adults, some of us have lost our ability to play. In truth, we never lose it; we just don't use it as often as we once did. Make it part of your work as a lector, then, to develop your sense of play, especially your imagination. As Albert Einstein said, "Imagination is more important than knowledge."[5]

Here's how play and imagination can help you with emotion. As you read your text, imagine yourself in the position of the characters you are proclaiming. Once you're familiar with your text, you may find it helpful to quiet yourself, close your eyes, and really work on visualizing the scene from your text. Put yourself into the situation as deeply as you can. What does the space you're in look like? Is it a room? How big? How crowded? Is it outside? In a desert? In a garden? Are there trees? What's the season? Fill your imagination with detail. (This exercise is very similar to the use of active imagination in Ignatian prayer and Christian meditation.)

Imagine yourself as Paul, writing to the Romans, telling them to be hopeful. Actually, it will be more effective if you picture yourself as Paul, standing in front of the Romans and preaching to them. What do you feel? Can you feel the love you have for them?

Imagine yourself as God (yes, as lectors, this is part of our awesome responsibility). Job has been railing against you for thirty-seven chapters, demanding that you justify yourself. What do you feel as you begin your response? As we noted earlier, feelings in themselves are not sinful, so our feelings are also part of our reflection of God. That means there are no feelings we have that God does not also have. Are you *frustrated, angry, amused, weary*? Does the emotion arise naturally as you imagine the situation?

In a narrative text, you will need to imagine yourself as each character in the text. Go through the scene from Luke, imagining yourself as Jesus. You know where you're headed. You know what you want the disciples to understand. You know how hard the message is. Place yourself in the scene, praying in solitude. Does the emotion come up for you? Then go through the scene again imagining yourself as one of the disciples, and one more time as Peter. What feelings arise? Allow them to surface. The richer the detail, the more you will be able to have a real emotional response.

In his letter to Timothy, Paul is recalling in his own imagination the experiences of his life and his hopes for the future. You will need to do the same. Instead of simply imagining yourself as Paul writing (or, rather, *talking*) to Timothy, imagine what Paul is imagining: his long work in evangelization, being abandoned by his friends, being rescued by God, awaiting his reward, and so on.

You may find that the emotions that surface are different than the ones you chose based on the text. This is okay. As long as these emotions are justified by the text, then go with them.

After doing this exercise, go back to reading the text, out loud, the way you will proclaim it. Do the emotions come up as you proclaim in the same way they

---

5. As quoted by George Sylvester Viereck in *Saturday Evening Post* 26 (October 1929).

did in your imagination? Repeat this exercise a number of times, and the association with the text will become even stronger. This is a great exercise to take into prayer as well.

The imagination exercise is a very useful tool not only for connecting with the emotion of a scene but also with the intention and the characters in the scene. If you find it to be powerful, you may want to use it all the time, even when you are confident that you can convey the emotional content from the text and intention alone. It can be as much a part of your preparation as reading the Scripture commentaries.

Substitution

No matter how hard you try, imagination won't always give you the emotional response you need. In that case, it's time to break the glass on the emergency technique: substitution. When we can't get the emotion we want from reading the story or imagining ourselves in it, we can substitute in our imagination an actual circumstance from our own lives that produces the emotion.

For example, if imagining myself as Paul preaching to the Romans doesn't evoke the emotion of pastoral love that I'm looking for, I can substitute for the Romans a person I feel that kind of love for. In this way, substitution is very similar to the technique of specificity we covered in the last chapter. Imagining myself talking to a close friend, perhaps someone who has turned to me for guidance in real life, should evoke the feeling of love I'm looking for. It needn't be a person I would actually guide in the way Paul is guiding the Romans. As long as it's a person I care for similar to the way Paul cares for the Romans, the technique will work. It won't be an exact match, however, so you can see why this technique shouldn't be your first choice for developing an emotional response. This kind of substitution is sometimes called *personalization*. (Notice that although I'm trying to convey Paul's love for the Romans, I'm careful to choose someone who will evoke a *pastoral* love in me and not a *romantic* love.)

We may have to substitute more than just a person in the scene, however. We may have to substitute an entire circumstance. For example, if I want to connect with that feeling of betrayal that comes up in Paul as he remembers being abandoned by his colleagues, I need to recall a time in my life when I was betrayed. If I want to connect with God's feelings in response to Job, I need to recall a time in my life when I was being challenged even though I knew I was right.

Walking into an acting class in Chicago taught by Jane Brody, a prominent casting director, I was a bit surprised to see that she had written on the board: WE ARE ALL BROTHERS AND SISTERS UNDER THE SKIN. Was this a religion class? Her point, however, was that the only reason acting works at all is because we are all human. We all experience the same emotions, the same drives, the same needs and wants. I can relate to Hamlet because I, too, have been indecisive when faced with action; I, too, know the weight of responsibility when I face a life-or-death decision. It seems so simple we don't even think about it, but acting wouldn't work—in fact, there wouldn't even be actors, theater, or film—if we didn't all share the same emotions.

This is the principle that underlies substitution. If I am reading Ezekiel, do I know how it feels to prophesy to a faithless nation? Of course not. But do I know what frustration feels like when no one is interested in what I have to share? You bet! So I can proclaim Ezekiel *as if* I were speaking to my child, or a committee at work, or even a customer service representative who is completely uninterested in what I have to say. Make sure you choose a real circumstance from your own experience. If you try to create one, you're just compounding the problem by substituting one circumstance with which you have no experience for another.

Notice that none of these techniques requires you to practice *expressing* a specific emotion. Rather, they ask you to place yourself in a situation from which the emotion arises naturally. Even in a piece with multiple characters or multiple emotions, we shift through the changes naturally, just as we would when telling a story in our own lives. If the changes don't come, either they aren't supported by the text, or we don't have a strong enough image associated with the change.

Real emotion comes from real understanding. The more you learn about the text you read—through text analysis, Scripture study, context, and also through intention, imagination, or thinking "as if"—the more you will express authentic emotion.

Feeling emotion authentically, however, is not enough. If I'm not getting an emotion from an actor I'm directing, the actor may argue, "But I felt it!" "Yes," I'll say, "but I didn't see it." Our language reveals that we read emotions both visually and aurally: "I can *see* you're upset." "You *sound* happy today." Communicating emotion is just as important as communicating intent.

Paul wants the Romans to know he loves them as he teaches them; God wants Job to know he's amused by his questions; Peter wants Jesus to know he's confident in his confession of faith.

We need to make sure we're communicating emotion when we proclaim. Watch yourself and others expressing emotion. What are the physical cues that you get or give to communicate emotion? See if these cues are present in your proclamation as well. Eye contact is very important, since emotion is read largely in the eyes and face. Open up your eyes; don't squint. Lift your face forward when you look up from the text. Open up your body; don't hunch over the ambo. Strive to make yourself bigger than you are so your emotions can be more easily read. Feel free to share your feelings; this is not the time to be reserved and keep them to yourself.

The Gibberish Test

A great way to check to see if your emotions are coming though is to speak the text in gibberish. This is an advanced technique you can try after you've done more work on proclaiming with emotion. Gibberish is a language of made-up sounds, so instead of saying, "In the beginning, the earth was a formless void," you would say, "*Da na bahootay, la blah sikah bujay kal.*" In this way, you will get a feel for the dynamic of the text without words at all. Your communication will be *all* nonverbal, using only your voice and body.

In fact, if you want to take things one step further, speak the text in gibberish to someone else. The person listening won't know the story but should be able to pick up on the emotion and intent. If this isn't consistent with what you mean to convey, then you have some work to do on your nonverbal communication.

Raising the Stakes

If you're having trouble getting the emotion you desire, don't simply try harder. That's likely to lead to histrionics. Likewise, if you find yourself overplaying and your emotions are coming across as false, then you're probably trying too hard to *show* the emotions you've chosen instead of *having* them.

Remember, emotion is like a pink elephant. The moment I tell you not to think of a pink elephant, you can think of nothing but. However, if I tell you to think of a blue monkey instead of a pink elephant, the elephant disappears from your thoughts. The only way to stop focusing on emotion, then, is to focus on something else, and that something else is intention. If your intention is strong enough, your emotion should follow naturally from the work you do. If you need to use active imagination or substitution, that's fine, but that's all preparatory work, and the focus during your proclamation should be on your intention.

If you still aren't getting to your emotion, then *raise the stakes*. Our emotions tend to be heightened when we have much to gain or lose on the outcome of our intention. Being stuck in traffic is likely to annoy us at any time, but if we're on our way to a job interview or to propose marriage or to see our long-lost brother, then we're going to be really angry or frustrated. Losing sight of our two-year-old at a family party may cause momentary anxiety; losing sight of her in a crowded market would lead to full-scale panic. When the stakes are high for the success or failure of our intentions, then our emotions are heightened as well.

So how do we raise the stakes for our proclamation? We need to think of what will happen if we succeed or fail in reaching our intention. What happens if the community does or doesn't acknowledge God, or stop their infighting, or deny themselves? As much as possible, make the consequences of success or failure real, not only for the community, but for yourself as well: *This is the most important reading they will hear today, this week, all year, ever. This is my one and only chance to achieve my intention. If I don't get them to change, no one will.*

Always assume that there is a person in the community who is hearing this story for the first time. Better yet, assume that there is a person who is hearing the story for the only time. If you aren't connecting with that person, neither is the message! Remember, the stories we have inherited are about *the day something happened*; after centuries of editing, what we proclaim are the most important stories of our tradition.

Being Emotionally Truthful to the Text

It may seem disingenuous to manufacture emotions in the way I've described. It seems too actory, maybe. After all, it's not for nothing that the Greek word for *actor* is the origin of our word *hypocrite*. A priest once told me that he didn't always feel celebratory every single time he presided at Mass. Not surprising.

But he would "act" as though he did, and sometimes, before Mass was concluded, he really did feel that way. Nevertheless, it wouldn't serve the community very well if, instead of "acting" celebratory when necessary, he just allowed himself to express whatever emotion he felt as he presided. He put not only his mind, body, prayer, and talents at the service of the community but also his emotions.

O, Hark, Lo!

There's a key word that will tell you the author is calling for a heightened emotion. The word occurs throughout Scripture, especially in the Old Testament. The word is so simple and deceptive, you've probably breezed over it a dozen times in your own readings. That word is O.

O (or Oh) is a great word because it expresses so much. Whenever you see that word, you know you need to heighten whatever emotion you're expressing. It's not by coincidence that this word is most often heard in exhortatory texts. Look at how many ways it can be used:

❖ *Angry:* How long, O Lord? I cry for help but you do not listen! (Habakkuk 1:2)

❖ *Exultant:* Shout for joy, O daughter Zion! Sing joyfully, O Israel! (Zephaniah 3:14)

❖ *Authoritative:* Hear, O Israel, the commandments of life (Baruch 3:9)

❖ *Praising:* O Lord and lover of souls (Wisdom 11:26)

❖ *Plaintive:* Hear my prayer, O God (Psalm 54:2 NRSV)

❖ *Loving:* O my people, I will open your graves and have you rise from them (Ezekiel 37:12)

To see the power of this word, take it out of these phrases and see how they change. The word was put there for a reason. The author made a specific choice, so you need to make a specific choice about it, too.

O is your cue to bump up your energy and emotion. Think of it as a big space that you need to fill with emotion. And although it's a short word, you shouldn't pop it out like a dog's bark. You can linger over it; stretch it; make the community really feel the emotion it contains. Play with it in your mouth and with your voice and see what you can get from it. It's a gift!

Some other cue words that indicate heightened emotion include: *Lo, Hark, Alas, Woe, and Amen, Amen!* Exclamation points also indicate exhortatory text and heightened emotion. Since punctuation is determined by translators and editors, check a different Bible translation from your own, which may have exclamation points in different places.

Praying the Liturgy of the Hours may create a similar experience. The psalms, prayers, and readings chosen for a particular day may not fit the way I'm feeling that day, but as a part of the Church universal, I am praying with many people whose feelings the psalms express perfectly. Instead of praying out of my own feelings (which I can and should do at another time), I express the emotions of the community. I am sad with those who are sad, repentant with those who are repentant, joyful with those who are joyful, especially with those who can't express these emotions themselves. "Whenever we pray [the Liturgy of the Hours], we take on a universal voice. We are no longer an individual praying: we are the voice, body, and soul of the earth itself."[6]

In a similar way, when I proclaim and express an emotion that is not my own, I am serving the larger needs of the community. I am making present to them the emotion that is present in the text. If I read with the emotion I came with, or with no emotion at all, then I'm not being faithful to the text.

It's not easy. The emotion I see proclaimers express most often is *fear*: fear of expressing any emotion, or fear of going over the top when they do so. We strive toward status quo. Biologists teach us that all living things, as small as a one-celled organism and as large as the entire ecosystem of the earth, strive toward balance. When our emotions get too hot or cold, we try to correct this imbalance. That's why it can be uncomfortable to be emotional in our proclamation.

If this is something that is still very difficult for you, even after much trial, you simply may not be called to this ministry. It's nothing to be ashamed of. As easy as it looks, not everyone can be an actor. Not everyone can sing in a choir. And not everyone can proclaim. Just because we can read in front of people doesn't mean we can also bring emotional life to that reading. As we've seen, more skills than just reading skills are needed for this ministry. Someone who has no sense of rhythm will not make a very good choir member, even if they have perfect pitch.

Don't be too hard on yourself, though. Keep working at it, and ask others to assess whether they see improvement in your work. (See the next chapter for more on this.)

Eight Important Things to Remember about Emotion

1. Don't be timid about showing emotion in your proclamation. It's an integral part of Scripture and must be proclaimed along with the text.

2. Emotion may spring naturally from intention, but should still be checked against the text.

3. Choose an emotion that is complementary to the intention and that is supported by the text.

4. Don't be afraid of choosing a "negative" emotion if it is appropriate.

6. Ronald Rolheiser, *Prayer: Our Deepest Longing* (Cincinnati: Servant, 2013), 20.

5. Some texts, especially long texts and narrative texts with multiple characters, may have multiple emotions, even though they may have a single intention.

6. If, in your preparation, the emotion you've chosen doesn't flow from you authentically as you respond to the story, then use your *imagination* to place yourself in the story. Make your imagined scene rich in detail, and see if the emotions come for you.

7. If not, use the technique of *substitution*, and proclaim the story as if you were in a circumstance in your own experience that produces the emotion you need.

8. If the emotion you have is not being communicated, raise the stakes: make this the most important reading the community will hear, and yourself the only one who can proclaim it.

Chapter 7

Working on Being Real: Save the Ham for Dinner

The worst insult you can throw at an actor is "I didn't believe you." The ultimate goal for actors is to lose themselves so completely in a character that even their closest friends and family forget they are watching someone they know and believe they are seeing the character. "Don't let them catch you at it" is the proverb of the actor. Much of an actor's training is directed toward this goal of believability.

A false performance usually stems from one of two extremes: underplaying or overplaying. When we underplay, the audience doesn't see in us the actions, emotions, and energies they would expect from our character. The performance is flat, uninteresting, and hence unrealistic. When we overplay, we overdo these actions and emotions so they don't seem real. Too much attention is placed on the performer, and their performance overwhelms the character. Overplaying also results from emotions and actions that are believable in themselves but aren't believable in the context of the character's life and situation. In any of these cases, the audience is pulled out of the imagined reality of the play or movie. They know they are watching a performance instead of believing they are watching a real interaction.

 Early in his career, Harrison Ford was told by a studio executive that he had no future as an actor. When he asked why, the executive said, "When Tony Curtis first walked onscreen carrying a bag of groceries—a bag of groceries!—you took one look at him and said, 'That's a movie star!'" Ford replied, "Weren't you supposed to say, 'That's a grocery delivery boy'?"

Of course they *are* watching a performance, and there's the rub. For all the actor's striving to appear *real*, acting is *unreal* by its very nature. Although some schools of acting teach that the actor should forget about the audience and try to focus exclusively on the scene, the fact is that the audience is there! In addition, actors must deal with sets, costumes, cues, and all sorts of other elements of the theatrical arts. They may be required to act as though they were climbing a mountain in subzero temperatures when they are actually sweating under layers of costume and hot stage lights. Actors can't turn their backs to the audience or the camera even if it would be more natural in the scene. Film actors have to act some very intimate and emotional scenes with a camera a few feet away from their faces, a boom operator holding a microphone over their heads, and a bunch of lighting and electrical equipment (and accompanying crew members) surrounding them.

A lector faces similar challenges. Reading in front of forty or four hundred or four thousand people is not an everyday occurrence. Further, really proclaiming a text requires skills beyond those we use in everyday interactions. Thus, a lector is also put into an unreal situation with the goal of bringing the community into contact with a real, living, breathing word.

Focus

To deliver a performance under such circumstances, actors must learn to focus their attention away from this unreal situation and into the situation of the performance. That is, actors must focus their attention on the character rather than on themselves. When they do this, they can really believe that they are on a freezing mountaintop, that the flat root beer in the glass is a fine scotch, or that they are alone in a room filled with people, cables, and hot lights. The rule is "the character before the self."

There is a similar rule for lectors, and that is "the Word before the self." Unlike actors, lectors are not to forget that they are in a church or imagine that their community is really Corinth. Remember, lectors' intentions are always their own and are always directed toward their community. A lector is not performing "as Paul" or "as Jeremiah." Lectors are not trying to connect the community with Paul or Jeremiah or even with themselves as lectors; rather they are trying to connect the community with the life within the Word, the life within the message. In this, we take as our model John the Baptist, who diminished himself that the Word might increase (John 3:30).

Now, let's be honest: if you've volunteered to be a minister of the Word, there's probably already a bit of ham in you. That's part of why you're willing to get up in front of the community and do this. Acknowledge this as gift! There's nothing that says you shouldn't enjoy your ministry. In fact, such enjoyment is likely a sign that it's a ministry you're called to.

Be aware that this gift must be placed at the service of the Word. Your ministry is not your own; it belongs to the community. You serve at their discretion, and you serve for their benefit. It's not about you. When it gets to be about you, just as when it gets to be about the actor and not the character, the ham starts appearing on the table. Be truly humble before God and before your community.

This is not to say that you can pull back on your intention or emotion in your proclamation. On the contrary, this is where you *should* focus, most especially on your intention. This will keep the focus off you as the lector and will prevent both the self-conscious, underplayed reading and the overplayed, actory performance. (This is also a great way to take care of nerves, as we will see a little further on.)

Proclaim your intention and not your emotion, your intention and not your voice, your intention and not yourself. If you have trouble with this, you may need to raise the stakes. That is, you may need to make the intention more important to you so it can occupy your focus. You need to strengthen your image of the blue monkey (intention) so it completely blots out the pink elephant (emotion, self, performance).

Eliminating distractions will also help your focus. Make sure there are no surprises when you prepare to read. Even if you proclaim from the same ambo every week, check it before the service. You never know when an electrical cord has been run across the step or a banner has been hung in front of the microphone.

Do your sound check. Avoid wearing clothes or jewelry that might get in the way of your hands or arms or make it difficult for you to walk up steps (if you need to). Wear shoes that are comfortable and won't slip, squeak, or clack on any of the floor surfaces in your church. Bring glasses if you need them and have them accessible. When you get to the ambo, you should only need to focus on the Word.

Getting a Second Opinion

It's said that the lawyer who represents himself has a fool for a client. I think it could also be said that the actor who directs himself has a fool for a director. When I direct myself in a show, I always invite a trusted colleague into the rehearsals a few times before we open. They will see things that I can't because I'm in the show.

Actors can't judge the impression their performance makes for the simple reason that their eyes and ears aren't in the right position to see or hear themselves. Sometimes actors will work in front of a mirror, but I don't recommend this for lectors (or actors, either). It requires you to split your focus between proclaiming and critiquing, and you usually end up doing a poor job of both. Better to enlist the help of an honest and perceptive friend, preferably one who is a lector working on the same skills you're working on.

Jerry Lewis, who directed himself in a number of films, helped develop a video camera that fit inside a film camera, so he could see his performance immediately after a take and make appropriate adjustments. Even though he was aware of himself as he acted in the scene, he wanted to confirm that what he thought he was expressing was really what was being captured on film.

It's ideal when the person who works with you during your practice can also be present when you proclaim. In fact, it's always helpful to have someone in the assembly when you proclaim who can give you feedback. Use whatever suggestions or critique you receive from this person the next time you proclaim. They can help you with your sound check and answer the following questions for you.[1]

1. Was I going too fast? Too slow?
2. Was my diction clear? Could you understand the words I was saying?

---

1. You'll also find a one-page guide for assessing a proclamation on page 133. It is downloadable and printable at the URL provided there.

a. If not, work on placing your voice more forward in your head to improve diction.

b. Adjust the microphone if possible.

c. You may also need to work on your articulation. Overarticulate when you practice to become more distinct in your speech.

3. Did I vary my inflection? My volume?

4. Did the pauses and stresses help the reading make sense?

5. How was my movement to and from the ambo? Was my posture at the ambo open and inviting?

6. Did I make eye contact—with everyone in the space?

7. If it's a narrative text:

a. Was the story clear?

b. Could you see the scene I was describing?

c. Could you tell who the different characters were as they were speaking? Did you know who said what?

i. Make sure you've chosen a distinct intention and emotion for each character in the narrative. Raise the stakes for each of the characters.

8. If it's a didactic text:

a. Could you follow the line of reasoning? What do you think the author was saying?

i. If your listener didn't get the gist of the text, you may need to slow down or watch that your pauses are not breaking up single thoughts or combining multiple thoughts. Some didactic texts are tough to get in a one-time hearing.

9. If it's an exhortatory text:

a. Could you follow the line of reasoning?

b. What do you think the author was saying?

c. How important did this text sound?

i. If it didn't sound important, *raise the stakes*. Make this proclamation the most important you've ever done. Think, "The community must hear this message, and I'm the *only* one who can deliver it."

10. What is the central message you get from this passage?

a. It doesn't have to be the same message you've chosen for your intention. Remember, the Spirit works differently in each of us as we respond to the Word. Just make sure that *some* intention is coming across. If not, then you may have chosen an intention that isn't supported by the text. If you think you have, raise the stakes.

11. Did you feel connected with me as I proclaimed?

  a. If there didn't seem to be a connection, make sure you're making eye contact, especially on the significant passages. Make sure your face and body are open to the community. Also, try raising the stakes.

12. Did you sense any emotion in my proclamation? What was it?

  a. If no emotion seemed present, you should raise the stakes. (Notice a pattern here?) Give yourself permission to show emotion in front of the community. It's part of the Word you proclaim and will help them understand it. If an inappropriate emotion came through—if your listener felt you were angry, for example, instead of exultant—then strengthen the details of your imagined scene or your *as if*. Also, examine whether your personal emotion is coming through rather than the emotion from the text. If so, raise the stakes and focus back on the intention.

13. Did the emotion seem true, or was it underplayed (reading was flat) or overplayed (seemed inauthentic)?

  a. Everyone's opinion on what is overplaying or underplaying will be different. If you get the same feedback from a few trusted listeners, make an adjustment. Put the message before the self. If you're underplaying because you're nervous, look at the suggestions in chapter 9. If you're overplaying, you may be trying too hard. "Own it, don't show it." Focus on the intention and forget about emotion. Allow the Spirit to do more of the work and trust that your preparatory work will give the Spirit what is needed to work through your proclamation. Place your gifts at the service of the community and the Word. If you're underplaying or overplaying, focus solely on your intention and—*raise the you-know-whats!*

What a privilege it is to be the caretaker of the Word! What a responsibility it is to be the keeper of the story for our community! Lectors who understand that privilege and responsibility are the ones who work very hard to proclaim well; they do so not for their own glory but for the glory of God and the love of the community.

Six Important Things to Remember about Being Real

1. A false proclamation stems from underplaying or overplaying. In underplaying, no intention or emotion is communicated. In overplaying, the emotion seems too big or unreal in the context of the proclamation.

2. Put the Word before the self, the message before the messenger.

3. Maintain your focus by eliminating possible distractions from your environment.

4. Have a trusted friend or fellow lector give you feedback on your proclamation by observing you in practice, and also during worship.

5. If feedback indicates that you are underplaying, give yourself permission to show emotion and raise the stakes on your intention.

6. If feedback indicates you are overplaying, focus on your intention and not your emotion. Raise the stakes to help your focus. Allow the Spirit to work through you.

Chapter 8

Working on Stage Fright and Other Annoyances: Nerves Are Your Body's Way of Showing You Care

F ace it. You're going to be nervous when you proclaim. Public speaking tops the list of most people's fears. Even actors with decades of experience say that they often suffer from stage fright. But this isn't necessarily a bad thing. Your nervous energy is a sign that you want to do your best—that you care about your work. You don't get nervous when you don't care about the outcome of what you do, or when you're doing something you consider unimportant. For example, you'd be much more nervous talking to your boss about a raise than about the movie you saw last night. Being nervous about your proclamation, then, is a validation that you've raised the stakes for yourself.

Your nerves are also a sign that you're working hard on your proclamation skills. If you've been a lector for some time, you may find that after working with the exercises in this book, you're actually *more* nervous about proclaiming than you were before. Good! This means you're shaking up the complacency that comes from experience and really challenging yourself to move out of your comfort zone.

Reading is safe; proclaiming means taking risks. We all fear making fools of ourselves, especially when we're trying to express passion and emotion in public. We don't want to reveal too much of ourselves to others. But we need to allow ourselves to be vulnerable. We need to put our ego at the service of the word and of the community. If you're not at all nervous (perhaps a better term is *excited*) about your work, then you may not be really stretching yourself to proclaim.

Relaxation

You need to be relaxed, though, to minister effectively. Good energy is one thing; clenched jaws and tight voices are quite another. Relaxation doesn't mean, however, that you're ready to fall asleep. When you're relaxed, you're in a heightened state of awareness, ready for your task, present to your surroundings, and responsive to the Spirit. Athletes, musicians, and other artists describe this state as being *in the zone, in the moment,* or *experiencing flow.* I'll talk a little more about this in the next chapter. When you work to relax, you're not trying to rid yourself of all excess energy, you're just trying to redirect it.

 In fact, trying too hard to get rid of anxiety will increase your anxiety level. Once, before a show, I came across another actor sitting backstage with his eyes closed, listening to a guided meditation on relaxation. When I tapped his shoulder to tell him the curtain was about to go up, he yelled, "Hey, I'm *relaxing*, okay?" We both started to laugh; obviously, the meditation wasn't working.

Instead of focusing on getting rid of your anxiety, focus on channeling your nervous energy into the emotion you're trying to express. Remember, emotion is energy, and nerves are energy, too. So instead of being nervous, try being angry or frightened or joyous or loving. You can even tell yourself, "I'm full of love [or whatever emotion you've chosen]. The energy I feel is an enormous love for this community." If you focus on *redirecting* your nervous energy rather than *eliminating* it, you'll likely be more successful. Use the energy for your reading. Acknowledge that the anxiety you feel is due to your passion for the Word and your love for God and your community. You'll actually be less concerned about your anxiety and may end up being less anxious as well. Even if you aren't, you will be using that nervous energy in a more helpful way.

Remind yourself also that it's not about you. The Spirit is there to take care of you and your proclamation; ultimately, you are placing yourself at the service of the Spirit and the Word. Remember, "the message before the messenger."

Reframing your thoughts in this way may be helpful to you, but it's also good to tackle nerves with some physical warm-ups. Following are a few exercises actors use. They not only help rid the body of nervous energy, but they also ready the body for its work in performance. As such, they're useful even when you're not very nervous. Remember, like acting, proclamation is a physical ministry, so your body needs to be ready for and responsive to your task. I realize that these exercises may subject you to some strange looks in the sacristy, vestry, or vestibule. Although they work best if you can do them just before the service begins, you may want to find a quiet place to do them, away from others.

Shoulder and Neck Rolls

Your chest, shoulders, and neck muscles should be warmed up and loose, since these are the muscles most involved in supporting your voice. Roll your shoulders in a circle. Roll them both forward a few times; then roll them both backward a few times. Then roll them in opposite directions one way, then the other. Roll your neck, but don't roll it backward past your shoulders; this movement creates a dangerous friction between the vertebrae of your neck. Instead, drop your head forward and roll it to one side. When your ear is directly over your shoulder, lift your head up and drop it to the other shoulder; then continue the roll to the front. You can do some of your favorite tongue twisters (see pages 38–39) as you do this exercise.

Bend Over, Shake Out

This is a great warm-up, even if you aren't nervous. Bend over completely as if you were trying to touch your toes (it's not necessary to do so). Let yourself be loose, not rigid, in this position. Keep your head down, your nose pointing at your knees. (Lifting your head puts a strain on your neck.) Now shake yourself out, moving your arms and shoulders and neck. Shake everything. Make an *mmmmm* sound or a *brrrrr* sound as you do this to loosen up your voice as well. Then, slowly move back into an erect posture. Imagine that you're placing one vertebra on top of another very slowly and deliberately. You can also massage your face with your hands; really move your lips and cheeks around.

Count Down

Here's an exercise that's especially good if you're feeling tired or unfocused. Lift your right arm high and shake your hand ten times, as fast as you can, counting down from ten to one as you do. Then do the same with your left hand. Then raise your right leg and shake your right foot ten times; then do the same with your left foot. Go back immediately to your right hand, this time counting down from nine to one. Then your left hand, right foot, and left foot, from nine to one. Keep up the speed. Do the same sequence again, counting down from eight, then seven, then six, and so on down to one.

Shout It Out

This is a great trick for handling stage fright and nerves before a performance, but it may be a real challenge to do in public: scream! That's right; see if you can find a place to scream *aaaaaaaaaah*, without having someone call for emergency services. Seated in your car might be a good place, but it's even better if you can find a place to do it where you can get your whole body into it. Really move as you do it. Shout as loud as you can, but don't strain your voice. (It's less straining if you try an open *aaaah* sound rather than a high-pitched shriek.) This scream does two things, almost paradoxically: it releases the pent-up energy that is coming out as nervousness while giving you energy by increasing your heart rate and opening up your lungs.

 The value of these exercises notwithstanding, the single most effective cure for stage fright, bar none, is *preparation!* If you practice sufficiently beforehand, you'll feel much more confident when it comes time for you to proclaim. No reframing of nervous energy, warm-up exercise, or relaxation meditation will take the place of practice, practice, practice.

Mistakes

No matter how many times you practice a reading, you're going to make a mistake every now and then. You'll skip a line, mispronounce a name, leave out a word, transpose letters—we all make mistakes; it's as certain as death and taxes. It happens to actors all the time, too. You've probably seen those very amusing collected bloopers culled from television and movies.

Of course, film and television actors have the luxury of correcting their mistakes via a retake of the scene. Stage actors have no such advantage. I was once doing a reading of a short story when I flubbed a word. The mistake I made gave the line an unintended and, well, slightly risqué meaning. You can bet people in the audience started to titter, which was only natural. I went back,

A Code in da Dose

I used to have the unfortunate tradition of losing my voice due to a cold in the final week of rehearsal of a play. It was the inevitable result of not taking care of myself during the stressful weeks prior. I'm careful to do better now, and you should be, too. A lector with no voice is about as useful as an actor with no voice. You're especially vulnerable during the stress of a holiday or when preparing for a big event, and of course these are exactly the times when you want to be at your best if you're proclaiming at these important worship services.

But it happens to all of us, and, one day, you will have to proclaim with a cold or a stuffy nose. Here are a number of tips for the care and feeding of your voice at such times (and always, really):

❀ The best thing you can do for your voice (and your health, especially with a cold) is to stay well hydrated. Drink lots of water. The steam from warm drinks will help open your sinuses and relax your throat muscles; however, stay away from caffeine, which tends to dry you out. Stay away from alcohol, too, for obvious reasons, but because it also has a drying effect.

❀ Avoid very cold drinks as cold constricts tissues, and tightness is not what you need. Avoid milk and dairy products, which tend to increase mucus production. If you have a lot of phlegm, add a little lemon to your water to cut it.

❀ Don't clear your throat with the *ahem* sound; it's abrasive to your vocal cords. Instead, make a sharp *huh* sound from the back of your throat when you feel the need to clear your throat, or take a drink of water. (This is good advice at all times.)

❀ Work hard to place your voice forward in your head; see chapter 3 on projection. If your sinuses are stuffy, this may sound (and feel) a little funny, but it puts less strain on your throat.

❀ Use the exercises in this chapter to keep your shoulders, neck, and chest relaxed.

❀ If you have a morning proclamation, don't start talking immediately upon waking up. Instead, hum the lowest note you can sound. Raise the pitch of this note just a bit (about five half-steps, for the musically inclined) and continue the hum. After a minute or so of humming, open your mouth to an *ah* sound. This will warm your voice up slowly. This exercise works even better in a hot shower, which is another great help in loosening up congestion.

❀ Once you have warmed up your voice in this way, you should keep talking (unless you feel you're losing your voice) all morning. Talking is the best warm-up you can do for your voice, so find a reason to talk, even if it's to yourself. The first extended use of your voice for the day should not be at the ambo.

❀ However, if you really feel like you're losing your voice, then do the morning warm-up and go on voice rest until the liturgy. Before the liturgy begins, read through your reading once, aloud, at about half-volume, to warm up your voice just a bit.

❀ Ever wonder why opera singers wear scarves all the time? They do so to keep their throat muscles warm and relaxed to protect their singing voice. It might not be such a bad idea for you to do the same, especially when you've got a cold.

gave the correct reading, and moved on, stifling my own urge to laugh. Had I done so, it would have broken the scene I was creating in the reading.

The community will take its cue from you. If you make a big deal out of a mistake, it will be a big deal. If you fumble over a word and say, "I'm sorry, I meant to say . . . ," you immediately draw attention to the mistake. (You also draw attention to yourself as lector, putting the self before the Word.) If you discreetly correct it, no one will think twice.

Correct a mistake as soon as you notice it by going back to the word and repeating the line correctly from that point forward. If you've read an entire line before you realize you made a mistake earlier in the line, you can simply go back and read the line correctly, perhaps placing a slight emphasis on the corrected word. In this case, you may want to reread the line or phrase in its entirety, even if you made the mistake in the middle.

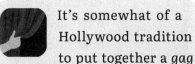

It's somewhat of a Hollywood tradition to put together a *gag reel* for a movie or television show, featuring the mistakes and behind-the-scenes antics of the cast and crew. Viewing the reel is usually the primary entertainment at the wrap party celebrating the conclusion of a shoot or season.

If you've gone a few lines past a mistake before you realize it, don't go back to correct it at all, unless you've significantly changed the meaning of the text. Remember, you have the advantage of having the text in front of you, but the community doesn't; they will likely not even know you made a mistake. (As I've said before, the community should not be reading along, they should be listening. If they are reading along, then, yes, they'll know you made a mistake, but they'll also know the correct reading.)

Most of all, don't let a mistake fluster you so much that you lose your focus for the rest of the proclamation. You'll be tempted to stay focused on yourself after making a mistake, so as soon as you correct the mistake, go back to your intention. Return your focus to the community: "I must get them to be hopeful!"

Whenever I've been onstage and made what I thought was a major flub, I invariably find later that no one in the audience even noticed it, so, really, don't worry about it.

Cold Readings

"Excuse me, but Anastasius hasn't shown up. Can you read the second reading today? I know you don't have time to prepare, but . . . ." Now what do you do?

Make the best of a difficult situation. You likely have at least a moment or two (or maybe a day) to go over the reading first before proclaiming. Your primary focus should be the text. Make sure you understand what the text is saying. You can read almost anything cold if you know what's being said.

Check pronunciations beforehand, but if you can't, don't stumble over a pronunciation you're not sure of. Instead, choose a pronunciation and commit to it. Say the name of a person or place like it's your closest friend or your hometown, and few people will even know whether it's correct or not.

If you have time, at least try to find an intention. One may stand out when you read it over. If not, then make your intention: "I want you to hear these words and take them into your heart!" Allow emotion to come naturally from this desire.

Did you know, however, that you actually can practice for a cold reading by . . . reading cold? Take some time every now and then to read something—anything—aloud, completely cold. Read from your copy of the lectionary or Bible, just to get more familiar with the language and structure. Read from your favorite novel, random websites, the owner's manual for your car. As you practice reading, also practice scanning the text and looking up to make eye contact. I know one actor who spent five minutes every day for a year reading something aloud completely cold. You can bet he got very good at cold readings.

Five Important Things to Remember about Stage Fright and Other Annoyances

1. Redirect your nervous energy into emotional energy. Use your excitement to give your intention passion and drive.

2. Relaxation is not a state of low energy but a state of focused energy.

3. Make sure your body is warmed up and ready for your task.

4. Reduce stage fright by being well prepared.

5. Don't make a big deal out of mistakes. Correct them and move on. It's more than likely no one even noticed.

Chapter 9

Putting It All Together: Practice, Practice, Practice—Then Get Out of the Way

When I first learned to play tennis, I was overwhelmed by all that I had to remember: Keep your eye on the ball. Follow through with your swing. Keep your shoulder down on your backhand. Stay on the balls of your feet. It seemed that, while I could remember to do some of these things sometimes, I could never remember to do all of these things every time. You may be feeling the same way after working through this book. We've gone through an awful lot of material, partly because, as I've said before, some techniques will work better for you than others. Nonetheless, there's a lot to remember. Here's some advice: forget it.

Okay, that's a bit of an overstatement. You shouldn't actually forget it, but when you proclaim, as much as possible, your focus shouldn't be on specific aspects of your preparation like inflection and gesture and eye contact and emotion. That work is really for your practice. If you've practiced enough, all those elements should be fully integrated into your proclamation by the time you walk to the ambo to read.

When I rehearse a play, my goal is to get the character so much into my bones that, should my brain be removed from my head on opening night, my body could still play the part! There are various ways to describe this: Athletes talk about *muscle memory* or being *in the zone*; artists speak of *flow* or being *in the moment*. When you're in the moment or experiencing flow, you're not struggling with pronunciation, rhythm, or eye contact. You're not working hard to show emotion. You're as comfortable with your intention as you are with where the microphone goes. Most of all, you're free to respond to the movement of the Spirit. The key is, you've worked on all these elements beforehand and now they're second nature. First nature, so to speak, is the act of proclaiming and being open to the Word flowing through you.

 Julie Andrews often quoted an adage she learned from her voice teacher: "Amateurs practice until they get it right; professionals practice until they cannot get it wrong."

Jane Brody, the casting director I mentioned earlier, spoke of actors being open to God's Spirit flowing through them and out toward the audience. God has the chance to communicate through the work of the actor, she said, if we will allow it. If this is true for the actor-artist, how much more valid is it for the proclaimer-artist? The goal of all the effort we put into our proclamation is to become an open vessel for God to speak to the community. Preparatory work doesn't get in the way of the Spirit; it actually gets us out of the way.

Trust that the work you've done in preparation and the work the Spirit will do through you will carry you through your proclamation.

This is a cooperative effort! Thomas Aquinas reminds us that "grace builds on nature."[1] You can't rely on the Spirit's help if you haven't done your own work, and your own work is insufficient without the movement of the Spirit. If you haven't prepared, don't expect the Spirit to show up at the last minute to save you. (It may happen, but don't rely on it.)

Practice, Practice, Practice

I know lectors who diligently begin preparing their Sunday proclamation the Monday before. This is good, but you may want to start even earlier. Of course, everyone is different. You may find it useful to practice for a few minutes a day every day for a few weeks; or you may want to put in a few hours all in a couple of days. My only caution is that you start early enough to allow yourself time to work out any problems or do any additional research you may need. You'll also want to sit with the Word in prayer. In general, I find that lectors don't spend enough time in preparation. Something like the following schedule might be the most productive.

When You Receive the Text

When you receive the text you're assigned, whether it's a week or a month before you're scheduled to proclaim, find some time soon afterward to sit down and read it through. (If your community doesn't assign readings until shortly before the service, let them know that giving lectors more time to practice will improve the community's worship, and ask if they might change the process.)

- ✣ At the first read, savor it and pray with it, as described in chapter 2.
- ✣ Then, allow the Word to sit with you for a few days; hold it in your heart. You may find words, phrases, or images coming up again as you go through your daily routine or as you return to prayer.
- ✣ After a few days, read it again. What resonates with you this time? Find some time to work with it in your imagination. Read and pray with it this way two or three times before you begin your more technical preparation. See if you gain any insights from the liturgies in the weeks leading up to your proclamation (especially if your reading is continuous or in a specific season).

One Week Before

Start your work on the actual proclamation. By now, you should have identified the style (narrative, didactic, or exhortatory). You may also have some ideas about intention and emotions.

- ✣ Read the contexts and the commentaries. Go over the other readings of the day. Make sure you understand what you're reading.

---

1. *Summa theologiae*, I, I, 8–2.

- Does an intention seem obvious from your readings and prayer? Consider the community context as well in choosing the intention. Are multiple intentions possible? In a narrative text with multiple characters, identify each character's intention. (See chapter 5.)

- What emotions do you identify as you pray or work with the text? Can you express these emotions as you read? If not, use the active imagination exercise or find an as-if situation to connect with the emotion. (See chapter 6.)

- Identify literary devices such as parallelism and paradox. Note choice words and emotion-filled words. Clarify pronunciations. (See chapter 2.)

- Try to paraphrase it. Which parts are easier for you to put into your own words and which parts do you still need to "own"? Try a casual read. Is your text good news? (See chapters 2 and 4.)

- What's the overall rhythm? Are there any places where the rhythm is prominent or interrupted? Where will you vary inflection and volume? (See chapter 3.)

- Does everything (emotion, rhythm, volume, and so on) support the intention you've chosen? Does your intention support the overall intention of God's Word to change the hearts of those who hear it?

Find some time to practice out loud at least once every two or three days in the week before your proclamation. If you get stuck or have difficulty with one part or the reading as a whole, try another technique. Continue to take the reading into your prayer as you work. If new insights come up for you, work them into your proclamation.

A Few Days Before

If possible, have a trusted colleague listen to your proclamation and offer feedback (see chapter 7). By now, you should be comfortable looking up from the text frequently to make eye contact with the community. Practice this as you read. Work on your intensity. Are you really bringing to your reading all you've discovered in your preparation?

At this point, let me warn you about a disquieting phenomenon familiar to most actors and other artists. I suspect it's familiar to anyone who undertakes a big project, in fact. Around this time in your preparatory work, you may think, "This is all too much. I'll never finish. I'll never make it to the end." You may come to a point where the work is proving difficult or too time-consuming or even too boring, and you'll be tempted to quit. After all, you may reason, what use is all this practice for a minute-and-a-half's work? What's especially seductive about this phenomenon is that you *have* already done a great deal of work at this point. Your temptation will be to give up, to leave things as they are, and to stop working. I urge you to push through this impasse and continue with your work. This challenge often occurs just as you are on the edge of a leap forward in your work, and giving up may prevent you from reaching that additional insight that really opens up your proclamation. You may not reach this point with every reading you prepare, but I guarantee it will happen sooner or later.

A Few Hours Before

Spend some time in quiet prayer. Do your vocal warm-ups (see chapters 3 and 8). Practice the text one last time before you leave home, so you can do so out loud and with your marked-up copy.

Before Worship Begins

Get to the church early, at least five minutes before you're supposed to be there. Being on time is one of the signs of a conscientious actor as well as a conscientious minister. Check the space. Do your sound check. Adjust the microphone if you'll be using it first. Consult with the presider or worship coordinator to see if there are any last minute changes or instructions. Attend to your energy; if you're nervous, acknowledge it and redirect the energy to your intention and emotion. Do some final vocal and physical warm-ups. Quiet your spirit in prayer and prepare to enter the service.

During Worship

Participate fully in the service: sing, respond, pray. As you approach the ambo, mentally repeat your intention to yourself: *I am going to get them to be hopeful! Just wait until you hear this message of hope!* Remember that your overall intention is to change the community so they conform completely to Christ!

During Your Proclamation

Announce the reading, and then pause briefly before you begin (see "First Looks" on page 60). Proclaim with passion, intention, and emotion! Let everything you've practiced come through, anointed with the grace of the Spirit. Allow the Spirit to work through you.

Hold for a significant pause at the end of the reading; hold the pause even longer if the reading ends very dramatically or emotionally, to let the moment sink in and allow the community to catch their breath. Then, if this occurs in your worship service, say the closing dialogue ("The word of the Lord"). Wait at the ambo for the community's response before you step away. Make sure you allow this to be the community's response; don't say it with them. After your proclamation, continue to participate in the service.

After Worship

Listen to any feedback from the community, from other ministers, and especially from any other lectors you may be working with. Consider unsolicited feedback carefully. Proclaiming, like any art, is open to interpretation, and no actor's performance or lector's proclamation is going to be without its critics. If the comments are consistent, take the matter to someone you trust. But, as the saying goes, if enough people say you look sick, you should lie down.

Three Important Things to Remember about Putting It All Together

1. Don't focus on the individual elements of your preparatory work during your actual proclamation. Trust that your work and the Spirit will carry you through.

2. The goal of all your practice and preparatory work is to get out of the way of the Spirit flowing through you during proclamation.

3. Start working on the text far enough in advance to fully integrate your preparation into your proclamation.

Chapter 10

Living the Word with Your Life: My Dear, You're Always On

Hollywood is a small town. Social circles and professional circles cross so much that deals are made at parties as often as they are in offices—perhaps more often. That person you run into at the grocery store might turn out to be the casting director you have an audition with this afternoon. Reputations get around quickly. Proclaimers, too, are in a very public ministry in a rather small community. When we stand in front of the community, we need to be conscious of the effect we have on others. Like it or not, we're in a position of leadership; we're an example for others to follow (1 Timothy 4:12).

Watch yourself during worship, especially on those days when you are ministering (and most especially if you're seated in the sanctuary). Are you participating fully? Are you enthusiastic in your responses? Are you singing? (You can't sing? Oh, yes, you can! I know a monk who says he has a dreadful voice, but he sings loudly and lustily anyway. "God gave me this voice," he says, "and I'm going to give it right back.") Are you attentive to the presider and other ministers? Are you reading along as Scripture is proclaimed? (You shouldn't be. Remember proclamations are listened to, not read!)

Living with the Word

One reason I prefer stage work to film is the length of time I get to spend with a role during a play. Although a movie can take months to film, each scene is shot only once (along with a number of retakes). In those same months, I can rehearse and perform a complete stage role many, many times. Though most of the work is done in rehearsal, even after a play opens I find opportunities to make my performance richer and more nuanced. Stage work allows an actor to really live with a character.

As proclaimers, we have the same opportunity to live with the Word. Perhaps you read a different passage of Scripture each day as part of your prayer. This is a wonderful way to know Scripture. But sometimes I find that one day isn't enough to really take the Word into my life. I like the idea of taking a week to ruminate over a passage of Scripture, to allow it to become part of my spirit. To be a person of the Word, you may wish to take each Sunday's Scripture (or at least the Gospel) into your prayer for the whole week.

A friend of mine is fond of "sticky-note meditations." He takes a phrase or idea from a reading and encapsulates it on a sticky note, which he then places on his bathroom mirror, his computer, or the dashboard of his car. The note reminds him all week of this particular idea. That way, he can meditate on it all week. He can bring it more deeply into his prayer. He can see how this idea plays itself out in his daily life. After all, this is where Scripture must have its effect if it has any effect at all: in our everyday life.

This is why I recommend working with a text for proclamation over the course of a few weeks rather than a few days. The longer you sit with the text, the more insight you'll likely have, and the richer your proclamation will be. You may find that the Word begins to infuse itself into your life in the way a character infuses itself into the life of an actor. When I'm in a show, I find phrases from my character popping up in my offstage conversations. In the same way, you may find that ideas from your text begin to pass through your thoughts and prayers as you prepare. Welcome this. Turn these ideas over in your mind. See what new insights come to you as this happens.

 An agent once told me a story about one of her clients, a young actress she was trying to market as a wholesome, girl-next-door type. One day, her client casually mentioned that she was planning on getting a tattoo. The agent tried to advise her against it. Tattoos did not fit the image she wanted to convey. Her client protested that she should be free to express herself however she wanted in her private life, but that she understood that when she was at an audition or a meeting with a director or producer, she would need to cover her tattoo. "I'll look how I'm supposed to look whenever I'm 'on,'" she said. "My dear," the agent responded in that mother-hen voice they all seem to have, "you're always 'on.'"

Living Out the Word

I asked a director I know to look at an early draft of this book. She commented, "It's not for the faint-of-heart, is it?" Well, no, I guess it isn't. Proclaiming is hard work, just as acting is, and, just as in acting, you need a spirit of passion and enthusiasm to get you through it. If you've found parts of this book challenging, I hope you haven't found them impossible. And most of all, I hope you've found them helpful.

But there's one aspect of proclaiming I'm afraid I can't help you with. I can't give you a technique or tool to make it work for you because it's the part I have the most trouble with myself. It's the element I find more challenging than all the others combined. It's the acknowledgment that, as proclaimers, we're expected to be people of the Word whether we're "on" or not.

Simply stated, it's this: *the power of the word to transform lives must begin with the life of the one who proclaims it.*

What I'm speaking of is *conversion*. We sometimes think that conversion is a personal experience that happens once in our lives. But conversion is ongoing. We are called to take up our cross *daily* and follow Christ (Luke 9:23). And this ongoing conversion experience is not only about Jesus and me. It is a social conversion as well. My conversion needs to fuel the community's conversion, and the community's experience needs to shape me. This is why proclamation is so important, because only in public proclamation can the Word call the entire community to conversion. You may find that the more you work on proclamation, the more you'll hunger for that relationship with God and with your community, and the more you will be called to conversion over and over again.

You already know, I suspect, the techniques you need to work out this conversion: a private and a public prayer life, a community to support you and hold you accountable, the nourishment of Scripture and tradition. I can offer no more.

I can only pray that God will grant you the strength and courage to respond to this call to conversion and will grace you with a zeal for proclaiming it in worship, with your life, and to the world, so that the Word may shine forth from you like light from a city set on a hill (see Matthew 5:14).

So there they are—ten things a lector can learn from an actor when proclaiming Scripture. In the next chapter, I will provide suggestions for reading other texts during liturgy (intercessions, for example), and the final chapter is addressed to those who train lectors. Thank you, proclaimers of the Word, for letting me help you with your ministry. May God ever bless you and all those you minister to. Amen.

Chapter 11

Other Duties as Assigned

As a minister trained in public proclamation, there are some other situations where you might be asked to share your gifts.

Intercessions

Many Christian liturgical traditions—Catholic, Episcopal, Lutheran, Methodist, and others—include communal intercessions in their worship services. These prayers are read by the deacon or a lay minister, usually a lector. This is entirely appropriate, since, as the community prays the intercessions, "the liturgy of word has its full effects in them."[1] The different names given to these prayers—prayer of the faithful, prayers of the people, general intercessions, universal prayer—all indicate that these are the prayers of the whole community, the whole Church really, rather than the prayers of any individual. This is an important distinction to keep in mind not only for those who compose the prayers, but also for lectors who proclaim them. In fact, it is your proclamation that allows the community to make these intercessions their communal prayer.

If you are to read the intercessions, ideally, you'll have received the texts at least a few days prior. If not, be certain to arrive early enough to spend some time reviewing them before the service. As with unfamiliar names in Scripture, check pronunciations beforehand, but if you can't, don't stumble over a pronunciation you're not sure of. Instead, choose a pronunciation and commit to it.

In most liturgical traditions, the presider begins the intercessions with a brief introduction and concludes with a closing prayer. You and the presider lead these prayers together, so arrive at the ambo before (not during) the presider's introduction, and remain standing there until the presider's prayer is completed, then return to your place.

The key to proclaiming these intercessions is to understand that they are indeed *prayers* of intercession—not narratives, not teachings, not announcements. Your goal is to allow the community, and *you*, to truly pray these intercessions.

Intercessions are most often constructed in one of three formats: "*For* something something . . . " or "*That* something something . . . " or "*For* something, *that* something . . . " The intercession then ends with a prompt ("we pray," "we pray to the Lord," "Lord hear us," and so forth), which invites the community to respond. This structure gives the intercession its rhythm. In the first

---

1. Introduction, *Lectionary for Mass*, 30.

two constructions, the first phrase is usually short enough to be proclaimed without a pause. In the "For . . . , that . . . " construction, take a short pause before "that." For other constructions or longer intercessions, use punctuation and the suggestions in chapter 3 to determine where to pause.

Take a *significant pause* after proclaiming the intercession and before the prompt. This silence allows the intercession to become the prayer of the community, giving all present the opportunity to take the intercession into their heart, join it to their own prayer, and then respond with the common invocation. When this pause is eliminated or rushed, the intercessions become a stream of words instead of prayer (Matthew 6:7). And let the community's response be their own; don't say it with them.

Pay attention to the same proclamation techniques as with Scripture: pacing, volume, inflection, posture, emotion, and intention. Eye contact is especially important, to invite the community into the prayer.

As noted above, your intention is to make these intercessions the authentic prayer of the community. As such, direct the texts not toward God but toward the community. Your intention might be taken from the text itself: "Let *us* pray. I want you, this community, to take on your responsibility for this prayer, to be people of prayer." The action you want from your community is "Pray!"

Emotion, too, is part of these prayers. Many of the intercessions will be sober, as they should be, recognizing the great needs in our world—poverty, violence, injustice, illness, death. It would be natural to proclaim with sadness or concern, but don't fall into this trap. Rather, pray with a sense of *hope* and *confidence* in God's care. We pray because we are people of hope.

In praying these prayers, the people exercise their baptismal priesthood,[2] an awesome responsibility. Perhaps nowhere else in the liturgy is our responsibility as a community so clearly demonstrated, reminding us that Word and Eucharist are not for our private edification and sustenance, but to equip us for service to the world. *That* is the reason you proclaim.

Responsorial Psalm

The psalms were written as songs. Thus, the responsorial psalm should be sung by the psalmist (the cantor who chants or sings the psalm) and the congregation.[3] However, at a weekday service or other celebration, or when a psalmist is not available, a lector should proclaim the psalm. Prepare for the proclamation in the same way you would with any text. Psalms are exhortatory texts, full of heightened emotions like exultation, love, longing, anger, frustration, and lamentation. Make sure you bring all of these emotions to your proclamation.

---

2. "In the Universal Prayer or Prayer of the Faithful, the people respond in some sense to the Word of God which they have received in faith and, exercising the office of their baptismal Priesthood, offer prayers to God for the salvation of all" (*General Instruction of the Roman Missal*, 69).

3. "It is preferable for the Responsorial Psalm to be sung, at least as far as the people's response is concerned. Hence the psalmist, or cantor of the Psalm, sings the Psalm verses at the ambo or another suitable place, while the whole congregation sits and listens, normally taking part by means of the response" (*General Instruction of the Roman Missal*, 61).

Your inflection should be especially broad, as befits a text that is meant to be set to music.

When you proclaim the response at the beginning of the psalm, take your time so that the community can commit it to memory. Although I usually recommend against saying a response with the community, the psalm response is an exception as it's often too long for a community to recall word-for-word. At the end of each strophe (verse), take a significant pause before inviting the community to proclaim the response. Raise your hand in invitation so the community knows they are to respond. Then proclaim the response with them confidently and deliberately. Don't mumble along quietly as if you weren't sure whether you were supposed to be helping them remember. Maintain eye contact with the community throughout the response, if possible; you may need to memorize the response yourself so you don't have to look down, or at least memorize the first few words or phrase so you can make eye contact as you invite them in.

In some celebrations, the psalm response is sung or chanted, led by a cantor or choir, and the strophes are proclaimed by a lector. For this to go smoothly, it's very important that the lector and cantor or choir meet beforehand to rehearse the psalm together, especially since during the service the lector will usually be at the ambo while the cantor will be leading the response from another location. In this arrangement, it's best not to sing the response with the cantor and community.

Gospel Acclamation

You may be asked to proclaim the verse before the Gospel, although if the Gospel acclamation is not sung, it may be omitted.[4] This verse is usually taken from Scripture, sometimes as a paraphrase, and is often exhortatory. Just because the verse is short doesn't mean it doesn't deserve a good proclamation. The response "Alleluia" really begs to be sung, so proclaim with brio without shouting it. Use heightened energy, emotion, and inflection, and, of course, smile! The same goes for other acclamations that might be used—during Lent, for example. They are still exhortatory antiphons, designed to signal the high point of the Liturgy of the Word, the reading of the Gospel. If the acclamation is sung by a cantor and the verse proclaimed by a lector, then get together with the music ministers beforehand to practice.

Commentator

Although the role of the commentator is still described in liturgical documents, it's rarely used in most churches. The role was more prominent in Catholic communities after the liturgical reforms of the Second Vatican Council, when the assembly needed guidance and explanations about the liturgy. The only function of the commentator that remains in most communities is the reading

---

4. *General Instruction of the Roman Missal*, 62.

of announcements, but this is usually done by a lector or the presider. If you're assigned this function, be sure to review the announcements in advance. Well-written announcements should be brief but inviting; in a culture in which we are all constantly connected, it seems pointless to read a litany of dates, times, and locations. Better to use this opportunity to pique the interest of the assembly and direct them to the community website or social media for details. In fact, let that be your intention when you read these: "Hey, check this out! Here's something fun, or enriching, or challenging!" "Be engaged" can be your action. And don't forget to smile!

Other Services

There are many other occasions for the proclamation of Scripture in which a lector might be asked to minister or wish to volunteer—Morning Prayer and Evening Prayer; sacramental celebrations like baptisms, reconciliation services, anointings of the sick; liturgies of the Word for the homebound; retreats; prayer services; and so on. Some communities offer the services of their trained lectors to proclaim at weddings and funerals. Wherever Scripture is proclaimed, you are equipped to contribute. If you're asked to serve at any of these celebrations or if you wish to volunteer, the same techniques and suggestions for proclamation apply. Just remember that depending on the service, you might not be proclaiming from a lectionary, so some of the cues that a lectionary layout provides—sense line divisions, opening and closing dialogues—may not be present. You'll need to account for that in your preparation. In these circumstances, if you're not reading from an actual Bible, any sheets of paper from which you proclaim should be placed in a dignified binder.

Chapter 12

The Care and Feeding of Lectors: Advice for Trainers

Over the years I've been privileged to train hundreds of lectors, and the techniques I've found most effective make up the content of this book. If you're responsible for training lectors, I think you'll find the techniques useful in your work as well. In this section, you'll find some additional suggestions.

Let's get one thing straight first: Lectors must be trained! This has been echoed again and again by John Paul II,[1] Benedict XVI,[2] and Francis.[3] So I continue to be surprised by the number of communities that provide no training, or limit it to the "policies and procedures" of their particular community. It's unfair to the community, and to the lectors as well, to ask or allow someone to become a lector simply because they know how to read and are willing to serve. Even those who might already be accomplished public speakers in their professional lives need to be trained as lectors. As evidenced in this book, although proclaiming draws on many of the same skills as other professions, these skills must be applied to the proclamation of Scripture in specific ways. Not only should lectors be trained before they serve, but there should be regular opportunities for them to come together to work on improving and deepening their skills.

 Academy Award winning actress Olympia Dukakis once said, "I'm always studying something: voice, singing, different disciplines with the body, clowns, masks. There's always something going on; it never ends." She was eighty years old at the time.

A Training Curriculum

I recognize that time is often limited for training. If possible, though, rather than a once-a-year, ninety-minute session, I'd suggest a multiple-session approach or a series of in-service seminars, each of which focuses on one or two skills. Some skills—such as voice, intention, and emotion—are significant enough to be worked on in multiple sessions. Also, I recommend that lectors be allowed to work on the skills at home, after they've been introduced, and then come back for a follow-up session to fine-tune, discuss problems, and check their progress. After all, this is how lectors work on their readings most often: at home, by themselves.

Another option is a day-long retreat and seminar, which would allow for four or more hours of training in addition to time for prayer and reflection. In

1. *Mane nobiscum Domine*, 13.
2. *Verbum Domini*, 58.
3. General Audience, January 31, 2018.

this format, you could break lectors into small groups to help each other, preferably in different spaces to allow for real proclamation without disturbing other groups.

The arrangement of chapters in this book can be used as a syllabus for training sessions. Your first, and perhaps most important, job is to help them understand the significance of their ministry (chapter 1). You'll be asking them to spend a lot of time and energy in this work—more, possibly, than they expected when they volunteered—to move from being readers to proclaimers. Only when they understand their role as ministers who make Christ present to the assembly in the Word will they be motivated to do the work you're asking of them.

Spend some time on the basics of text work, vocal technique, and body work before moving on to intention and emotion. Although it's true that effective use of intention and emotion provides a natural impetus for things like volume, inflection, eye contact, physicalization, and so forth, these basics shouldn't be ignored. The best actors are those who have a good handle on these foundational skills and work on them constantly; their voice and body become fine-tuned instruments from which they can play any intention and emotion that might be called for. Likewise for lectors, this basic work "stretches" our instruments so that we can proclaim whatever the reading demands—even when—especially when—it's something outside our comfort zone.

After introducing work on text, voice, and physicalization (chapters 2, 3, and 4), you could ask them to go home and prepare a reading (maybe one they will be proclaiming soon) using these concepts. Have them read the text and commentaries, identify the style and any literary devices, and begin to get the reading into their voice. They should be focusing on pronunciation and articulation, pacing, and varying volume and inflection. Ask them to note any problems, and in the next session, give each of them a chance to proclaim their reading. Even before working on intention and emotion, lectors should be able to see their proclamations improve with this work.

Dedicate considerable time to intention (chapter 5) and emotion (chapter 6); they are both critical to proclamation and take some time to work through and understand.

Some lectors think they need to find the *correct* intentions or emotions and might look to you for the answers. Emphasize that each of them should make their own choice; there is no one right answer as long as it's supported by the text. Even different lectors working on the same text can come up with different intentions and emotions.

Questions are a great way to help lectors with intention and emotion: "What do you think Paul is saying here?" "What does Jeremiah want from the community?" "What do *you* want from *us*?" "What is Isaiah, or Peter, or God feeling here?" "How might you feel in this situation?" "How have you felt in similar situations in your own life?" Then help them strengthen their chosen intentions and emotions by asking: "What do you want the community to do or to be after hearing this reading?" "Can you make the intention shorter, more direct, a command from you to the community?" "That's a good emotional choice; what about making it stronger?"

Remember that the Spirit will work within the hearts of the community to bring to light whatever intention each person needs to hear. But if no choice is made on the part of the lector, then the reading will be lifeless, and the Spirit's work will be impeded. In fact, I will usually not ask a lector about their choices until I've heard them proclaim the reading. If the reading is alive and full of emotion and energy, then their choices are clearly working. If the choices are not appropriate it will show up as reading that seems flat or false.

Feel free to challenge lectors, in a helpful way, if you think the intentions or emotions are not supported by the text—"Tell me what in this reading says what you're trying to say." "What are the emotional words in the text that support that emotion?" "What do you think is going on here, in the hearts of the writers or the characters?" You can offer tentative suggestions if necessary: "I hear God's mercy in this." "There are a lot of 'fear' words in this text." "It sounds to me like Paul is very angry here." This can help a lector modify the intention or emotion appropriately. Sometimes, though, a lector has found something in the text that I hadn't noticed until they helped me see it.

When I'm discussing intention with actors I'm directing in a play, for example, they will often come up with intentions for their characters very different from what I had in mind, but they can still work (as long as they can be supported by the text). In fact, I often see my intention in their portrayal even though I know this isn't what they have in mind. This demonstrates the power of having *some* intention, *any* intention, rather than no intention at all. The same is true for lectors.

As I've stressed, lectors need to be students of Scripture and liturgy, so you'll want to include these topics in your training. In addition to a broad overview of Scripture and alerting them to some good Scripture study resources, what I find lectors need most is guidance on how to do their own research on the many different texts of Scripture they will be proclaiming. The internet puts an overwhelming amount of information at our fingertips within milliseconds, but it's frequently not deep or appropriate. Lectors will appreciate help on how to assess quality and to identify what will be most beneficial to their work. See the Helpful Resources section for recommendations.

The goal of liturgical formation, the introduction to the *Lectionary for Mass* states, is "to equip the readers to have some grasp of the meaning and structure of the Liturgy of the Word and of the significance of its connection with the Liturgy of the Eucharist."[4] All liturgical ministers need a heartfelt connection to and understanding of the liturgy to which their ministry contributes, so you may wish to coordinate with the other liturgical ministries in your community to provide this training for everyone.

Lastly, you will, in fact, need to include some training on the "policies and procedures" of the worship service in your liturgical space—where to sit, how

4. Introduction, *Lectionary for Mass*, 55.

to move, and so on. I've included some suggestions on these logistical questions below, but one topic to be sure not to forget to cover is an introduction to the sound system. Not many communities can afford to hire a professional sound engineer to be at every worship service, so you need to become the sound system expert for your lectors. Learn everything you can about the system—especially about the best placement for the microphone at the ambo. You might have to learn mostly by your own trial and error, or you might be able to find a professional —for hire or as a volunteer—who can train you and other users on the system. Then you can, in turn, train your lectors.

Effective Coaching

Allowing each lector to get up and read and providing them with on-the-spot coaching is the real value of in-person training. I love to see how just a slight adjustment or suggestion makes a tremendous difference in a proclamation. And when lectors who are watching can see the change as well, it can be especially powerful. They're more inclined to apply these techniques to their own proclamations.

Ideally, conduct the training in your community's worship space so that lectors can use the actual set-up they will use in a service, including the microphone. As lectors read, stand far back in the space to check projection—not only of their voice, but also their expression. Can you see their eyes? Can you hear them clearly and distinctly? Are they using the sound system effectively? (Keep in mind that the acoustics of a mostly empty space will be different from one that's full of people.) Standing far back is also a way to remind lectors that they should raise their energy and strive to connect with those furthest away from them in the congregation.

Listen to the proclamation with fresh ears. You may know the reading well yourself, but try to listen as if you were hearing it for the first time. Don't look at the text during the proclamation! Pay close attention to the lector with your eyes and ears. If you miss a word or phrase, help the lector understand the problem. If you want to jot down any notes, make them quick and ideally do it after the proclamation is finished.

After a lector has read once, I start my coaching by asking them, "How did that feel?" or "How did that go for you?" Very often the lector will identify some of the same strengths and challenges I noticed.

As you make your comments, make a "sandwich" with your feedback. First, comment on what worked, then give any suggestions for improvement, and end with an affirmation of the lector's work, perhaps calling out what was most effective in the attempt. Have the lector try the reading again, right away, while the suggestions are still fresh. There will almost always be an improvement due to, if nothing else, reading it a second time, which at least demonstrates the value of practice! But there should also be some specific improvements based on your suggestions. If there aren't, then the person might not have understood your suggestions, or they may have become more self-conscious. Some lectors need time to internalize recommendations; likewise, some techniques require thought and practice before they can make a difference. As the lector sits down, offer some final affirmations of their work.

Don't fall into the trap of offering only positive feedback for fear of losing a volunteer! Affirmation is important, but if that's all you give, you won't be trusted. In fact, each of your lectors is probably an expert in some area in their own life and likely has experience giving helpful critiques to others based on their expertise. You are the expert when it comes to proclaiming, so own that. Most everyone knows that there is always room for improvement, and is eager to learn.

Make sure you give critiques in a way that's helpful. You might have heard the term "actor's director." This is a director who understands how to give direction that actors can use. It can be frustrating to work with a director who gives only technical directions ("Raise your voice slightly on this word. Look to the left on this line.") or one who talks in very general terms ("You need to be more angry.") The best directors work *with* their actors, coaxing a performance from them that sometimes the actors themselves didn't know they had in them! Thus, instead of simply *telling* lectors what changes they should make, help your lectors use the techniques and exercises in this book to *bring about* these changes. Chapter 7 provides a guide for reviewing a proclamation, along with cross-references to the techniques that can help in specific situations.

As I noted above, questions can be a great coaching tool. Instead of saying, "You need to convey more of the hurt Paul is feeling here," ask, "What might Paul be feeling here? How would you feel in this situation?" Questions like these allow the lector to come up with their own answer rather than trying to force someone else's interpretation onto their proclamation, which often comes across as fake. A dozen lectors all working on the same reading could well come up with a dozen different ways of proclaiming it—and that's fine—as long as each proclamation can be supported by the text. That variety shows the richness of the Scripture with which we work.

Avoid giving "line readings"—don't demonstrate what you're looking for by proclaiming some or all of the reading yourself. Sometimes inexperienced lectors (and actors) will ask for line readings, but emphasize that, to be authentic, the proclamation needs to be their own, not a mimicry of someone else's.

Ensure that you have enough time for each person to have at least one opportunity to read, receive coaching, and read again. To allow this, you may consider offering multiple training sessions with smaller groups. You can also break a larger group into small groups and have them work on coaching each other. If you do this, first have a few lectors read in front of the whole group while you demonstrate how to coach. The short form for reviewing a proclamation in the appendix may be helpful for this situation.

Training Lectors to Help Each Other

Lectors can support each other effectively only when they share a common goal and a common language to achieve that goal. Your community's lectors should all understand that the goal is proclamation rather than reading, and they should be able to recognize the difference. They need to be familiar with the concepts and techniques in this book and be able to discuss style, literary devices, inflection, tempo, physicalization, intention, emotion, and so on.

In your training sessions, model the way you'd like them to work with each other. You might point out how to sandwich suggestions with affirmations. Some might not be comfortable identifying areas of improvement for other lectors. When I have lectors work with each other, I'll challenge each person to identify at least one thing they thought went well and one thing that could be improved for each reader.

Lectors can continue to help each other after training. When more than one lector is assigned to the same service, for example, they can give each other feedback afterwards. Again, the short review form in the appendix will be helpful for this purpose. Some communities ask lectors to meet regularly in small groups and work on upcoming proclamations. These meetings could also include some time for Scripture study or sharing focused on the readings. Other liturgical ministers—cantors, musicians, Communion ministers, homilists and preachers—might be invited to that portion of the meeting as well.[5] Gathering lectors together to practice is a wonderful support, especially in a ministry that can be solitary. Just ensure that everyone has a chance to practice their readings aloud (preferably standing up!) and to do so multiple times.

Troubleshooting Guide

Many of the issues or problems with proclamation can be addressed using the concepts and techniques already presented in this book. There are, however, a few situations that might arise in training that deserve mention:

Pacing

I'd say one out of every three or four lectors needs to *slow down*. If I notice a lector reading at too fast a pace, I'll usually stop them right away and ask them to restart and go more slowly.

Difficult to Understand

No reading can be effective if it's not understood by the community, but it's not helpful to simply say, "I couldn't understand you." Rather, be specific. Which parts of the reading were difficult to understand and why? Make sure the lector is going slowly enough. Many comprehension issues can be resolved just by slowing down. Did they pause in appropriate places or fail to pause where needed? Work on articulation if necessary. You might suggest that a lector overarticulate

---

5. "How good it is when priests, deacons and the laity gather periodically to discover resources which can make preaching more attractive!" Francis, *Evangelii gaudium*, 159.

as they practice, at least on certain phrases or passages that are problematic. Watch for the dying inflection (see chapter 3). Remember also that nonverbal cues provide more meaning than words themselves. If the lector is not attending to nonverbal communication (inflection, pausing, pace, facial expression, tone, body language), if it's not strong enough, or not a match for the words, then the reading will be more difficult to understand. Eye contact, too, aids comprehension, as the eyes are where much of nonverbal communication is read, especially emotion. See chapter 4 for more on improving eye contact.

No Eye Contact

Whenever lectors won't look up or look up very infrequently, a couple of different things might be going on. First, they might be afraid of losing their place in the reading. If it improves their eye contact, they can discreetly use their hand to mark their place in the reading and slide it down the page as they proclaim. Second, stage fright can make it difficult for lectors to look up, as seeing the assembly makes them even more nervous. Eye contact also requires some vulnerability on the part of lectors, especially when they are sharing emotions. If the technique of looking just over the heads of the assembly or the other exercises in chapter 8 don't relieve them of their fear, then perhaps this ministry is not for them. There's no reason anyone should be forced to do something they clearly don't enjoy!

Flat Reading

This is one of the most common issues and, of course, most of the techniques and exercises in this book are designed to address this. But even lectors who really want to proclaim and who have done all their preparatory work will rise to the ambo and still give a flat reading. As a trainer, here are some ways to help:

❈ Make sure their technical foundation is firm: appropriate tempo, varied use of inflection and volume, good posture open to the community, frequent eye contact, and so forth.

❈ Usually, a flat reading can be improved with work on intention and emotion. They may need to choose a stronger intention. Make sure their intention is directed from them to the community. Help them choose an intention that moves the community to action ("What do you want us to do or be after hearing this?") and is expressed as a command: "Be hopeful! Trust God! Repent!" Have them proclaim again with only that one thought in mind. Ask them to focus on nothing else but that command.

❈ In the same way, help them choose stronger emotions. If they've chosen fear, for example, prompt them to make a stronger choice that fits the text, such as terrified, anguished, distraught, and so forth.

❈ If their choices for intentions and emotions are strong but they still aren't coming through in the proclamation, make sure they have raised the stakes (see pages 91, 94, 96, 98–100.). I'll sometimes stand all the way in the back of the worship space, arms crossed, scowling, and give them a challenge: "You need to convince me. Direct all your energy into getting me to change my mind and heart."

❖ The specificity exercise (see pages 67–68) is another good technique for raising the stakes.

❖ If emotion is weak or absent, guide them through the imagination or substitution exercises (see see pages 88–90). Ask them to spend time on these exercises at home. (They require focused work to bear fruit.)

❖ Lectors who are nervous or afraid will usually give a flat reading, especially when they are new to the ministry. The exercises in chapter 8 can help with stage fright, and practice, practice, practice will help reduce anxiety.

❖ Some lectors have trouble smiling when it's needed to communicate good news. I'll engage them in brief conversation about this or about those things in their life that make them smile and, inevitably, they'll break into a smile. I ask them to immediately proclaim again, taking that smile into the reading when it's called for. They learn quickly they *can* smile in their proclamation.

Over-the-Top Reading

Going over the top is a much rarer problem than a flat reading, but it does happen. Lectors may read slowly, overdramatically, with unnatural inflections or rhythm. They've lost the immediacy of the story they're telling and turned the reading into a performance that no longer seems like organic communication. The technique of *specificity* can help with this (see pages 67–68; 86–89). You can put this technique into action during training: Invite the lector down from the ambo to sit beside you and have a casual conversation; ask the lector to tell the story of the reading conversationally to you one-on-one, friend to friend. In this scenario, lectors might read from the text or tell the story in their own words. This usually has the effect of bringing their voice and energy level down to something more genuine and believable. When they've achieved that, have them immediately take that same energy up into the ambo and proclaim the reading again.

A caution: don't over emphasize this problem by warning lectors not to be too dramatic or not to turn their reading into a performance. If you do, all your lectors will likely pull back on their emotion or intention for fear of going too far; in fact, the ones who need to take more of a risk with proclamation will probably pull back the most. It's much easier to work with one or two who might go over-the-top than to stifle everyone from real proclamation.

Concerns about Proclaiming

Occasionally, I run across a lector who understands the importance of proclaiming rather than reading, but is anxious about trying it because it's so different from what the community is used to. Well, I say, you have two choices: you can do what the community expects, or you can do what the Word demands. While working with a group of seminarians, I asked them to recall an effective proclamation they had heard, and to identify what made it so. One seminarian recalled a lector who, hands joined in prayer in front of him, read the reading in a solemn tone without looking up. The seminarian explained that he thought this was effective because it showed the great reverence the lector had for the Word he was reading. Of course, I had a different perspective. At the end of our work together, and after seeing the difference it made in his own and others' readings, he agreed that true reverence demands real proclamation. This deeper connection with the Word, which the community is offered through real proclamation, ought to convince anyone nervous about "trying something different."

The Rubrics of Worship

In my training workshops, lectors sometimes ask me questions about the "right way" to do things in liturgy. I usually refer them back to their community's worship coordinator, since each tradition has its own style of worship, guided by liturgical rubrics. Based on my experience, however, I do have some suggestions, which I'll share here. I will mostly refer to the Roman Catholic liturgy and the rubrics contained in the *General Instruction for the Roman Missal* (GIRM), but readers from other traditions may find these thoughts helpful as well.

Scheduling

Ideally there should be as many lectors at a service as there are readings, apart from the Gospel.[6] Asking one lector to proclaim both readings in a service not only limits the diversity of ministers at the service, but also doubles the preparatory work for the lector!

Assign lectors well in advance, at least one month, so they have adequate time to prepare. Specify which readings will be used, especially when there are options in the selection of readings or when there are short and long forms. Make sure your lectors have access to copies of the readings exactly as they appear in your lectionary; remember that the readings in the lectionary may be different from the biblical text, even if it's the same translation. Lectors should check in with the presider or worship coordinator before the service to ensure they have prepared the correct versions.

If lectors are assigned to lead the intercessory prayers, they should be sent a copy in advance, especially when they are taken from a published text. Yet even if they are composed anew each week by pastoral leaders in the community, they could be sent or made available electronically a few days before, with the caveat that there might be last minute changes. Be sure to include phonetic pronunciation aids for any unfamiliar personal names that are included.

You might also invite lectors to volunteer to proclaim as needed at other services, such as weddings, funerals, baptisms, blessings, communal prayer, or to the sick and homebound. The proclamation of the Word is an important part of these celebrations, so it's entirely appropriate to assign trained lectors

---

6. GIRM, 109

to them.[7] Although family and friends are sometimes asked to read on these occasions, the option of using a trained lector could be appealing. Given that public speaking ranks high on the list of most people's fears, some might be grateful for the gift of a trained lector's participation! It also reinforces that these celebrations are not private events, but take place with the whole community as witnesses.

Dress Code

Let's be clear: God probably doesn't fret over proper church attire as much as we do. Ministers, including lay ministers, may wear an *alb*—the white robe which is the garment of all the baptized—or "other appropriate and dignified clothing."[8] Of course, what is considered "appropriate and dignified" varies by context, culture, and generation. What's appropriate for a service at a retreat house at the beach might be quite different from Easter Sunday in a cathedral.

Use care when establishing a dress code for lectors and other ministers. No one should be denied serving as a minister because of their clothing. This may seem obvious, but even simple requirements like suits or dresses could make some people reluctant to serve out of concern that they don't have the right clothes. Vesting ministers in an alb can help, but this also sets them apart from the assembly. Each community can decide on the most appropriate option.

A good rule of thumb is to consider how the assembly usually dresses for your services. Lectors and other ministers might dress up a notch from that but should not look so different that they no longer seem to belong to the community.

Opening procession

If no deacon is present, a lector carries the Book of the Gospels in the procession. Other lectors may walk in the procession, but I recommend this only if they will be seated in the sanctuary. Otherwise, it's appropriate for them to be seated in the assembly at the start of the liturgy. The GIRM states that the book is to be "*slightly* elevated."[9] A book held high over the head of the minister is not slightly elevated! In this position, it can distract from the cross, which has the place of honor and leads the procession. I recommend raising the book just below eye level, so you're looking right over the top of the book, not around the side or, worse, under. This height still conveys the respect we give to this book (we're not, for example, carrying it at our waist, resting against our chest, or under our arm!) If there is no one available to carry the Book of the Gospels, it may be placed on the altar before the liturgy. (If sufficient ministers are not available, the cross should be carried and not the Book of the Gospels.) Note that the lectionary is never carried in the procession instead of the Book of the Gospels,

---

7. Benedict XVI writes about the importance of the proclamation of the Word in celebrations outside of Mass in *Verbum Domini*, 61–63.
8. GIRM, 339.
9. GIRM, 194.

even if the Gospel is read from the lectionary. Although the rubrics don't specify this, the Book of the Gospels is not carried out in the closing procession.

Seating

Lectors are drawn from the assembly, and I recommend they be seated there, near the front, with easy access to the ambo. If the design of the space makes access difficult, they may sit in the sanctuary along with other ministers.[10]

Moving to the Ambo

When it's time to read, lectors should move directly from their seat to the ambo. Some communities ask lectors to bow to the altar before proceeding to the ambo, but this is not specified in the rubrics, and I recommend against it. For one thing, stopping in the middle of a direct movement is distracting to the community, who should be preparing to focus their attention on the ambo. This is especially true when lectors must go out of their way to get to the front of the altar. The rubrics only specify that the priest or deacon bow to the altar as part of the procession to the ambo with the Book of the Gospels, during which the whole assembly is rising to stand and singing the Gospel acclamation, preparing to receive the Gospel.[11]

Silence

The GIRM recommends a few moments of silence after the readings "so that all may meditate on what they have heard."[12] If you choose to include this, it's best facilitated by having the lector remain at the ambo in a prayerful posture (head bowed, hands on the ambo or folded at the waist) after the people's response. Otherwise the silence is disturbed by the comings and goings of the lectors, psalmists, and Gospel proclaimers as they move into their positions. The Church has long called for more silence in liturgy,[13] and in contemporary culture, it's a rare commodity. Silence may make the community a bit uncomfortable when it's first introduced, but eventually they'll come to value it.

Intercessory Prayers

The prayers should be read from the ambo.[14] As I mentioned in chapter 11, the presider and the deacon or lector lead these prayers together, so the deacon or lector should arrive at the ambo before (not during) the presider's introduction and remain standing there until the prayer is completed.

Closing Procession

The rubrics say very little about a closing procession, only that the priest and deacon withdraw "in a manner similar to the Entrance Procession"[15]. This doesn't mean, though, that the procession has to look like a mirror image of the opening.

---

10. GIRM, 195.
11. GIRM, 175.
12. GIRM, 128.
13. *Mane nobiscum Domine*, 13 and 18; *Verbum Domini*, 66.
14. GIRM, 71.
15. GIRM, 186.

The post-communion rite is very brief. It's all about getting the community out into the world. Our common worship should motivate us and inspire us to take what we have received into the world. There's almost a sense of rushing from the altar to the world; anything that slows this down is counterproductive. There's nothing wrong with having no closing procession at all; at the very least, it should be simple and quick, with only the presider, deacon, and perhaps the cross bearer participating. Even if other ministers seated in the sanctuary join the procession, there's really no reason that minsters seated in the assembly should do so. As noted above, the Book of the Gospels is not carried out in procession.

 A final note on these rubrics: as you train lectors, let them practice walking through all these movements. They can feel a little awkward for anyone new to liturgical ministry, and some will fear making a mistake or looking foolish. The more you can help your lectors get comfortable with the logistics of the liturgy, the more relaxed they will be in their proclamation.

A Quick Guide to Reviewing a Proclamation

General areas to review are listed below. Questions are provided to help focus comments. Be sure to indicate what worked, as well as making suggestions for improvement. See the chapters listed for an explanation of each focus area.

VOICE (chapters 2, 3): How was the tempo? Too fast or too slow? Were any words difficult to understand due to diction, pronunciation, or volume issues?

_____

_____

Were inflection (pitch) and volume varied as appropriate? Did the pauses and stresses help the reading make sense?

_____

_____

PHYSICALIZATION (chapter 4): How was the proclaimer's movement to and from the ambo? Was posture at the ambo open and inviting? Was there frequent eye contact with the community? Did the proclaimer smile as appropriate?

_____

_____

_____

INTENTION (chapter 5):

- ✤ For NARRATIVE texts: Was the story clear? Could you see the scene being described? Could you tell who the different characters were as they were speaking? Could you tell why the story was being told?
- ✤ For DIDACTIC texts: Could you follow the line of reasoning? What was the point of the teaching?
- ✤ For EXHORTATORY texts: What message was being communicated? Did it sound powerful and urgent?

_____

_____

_____

EMOTION (chapters 6, 7): What emotion(s) did the proclaimer express in the reading? Did the emotion seem true, or was it underplayed (reading was flat) or overplayed (seemed inauthentic)?

_____

_____

_____

OTHER COMMENTS (Continue on reverse if necessary.):

_____

This form can be downloaded at www.ltp.org/products/details/BRPW. From *Beyond Reading, Advanced Training for Proclaimers of the Word of God* by Douglas Leal. © 2022, Liturgy Training Publications, 800-933-1800. Text © Douglas Leal.

HELPFUL RESOURCES

Bibles

Catholic Study Bible, Third Edition. Donald Senior, John J. Collins, and Mary Ann Getty, editors. New American Bible Revised Edition. New York: Oxford University Press, 2016.

The Holy Bible: New Revised Standard Version, Catholic Edition. New York: Harper Collins Bibles, 2007.

New Oxford Annotated Bible with Apocrypha: New Revised Standard Version, 5th edition. Oxford University Press, 2018.

The New Jerusalem Bible. New York: Doubleday, 1990.

The Revised New Jerusalem Bible: Study Edition. Henry Wansborough, OSB. New York: Image, 2019.

Lectionaries

Ritual Editions

National Conference of Catholic Bishops. Lectionary for Mass for Use in the Dioceses of the United States of America. 2nd typical ed.

> Vol. 1, Sundays, Solemnities, Feasts of the Lord and the Saints, Year A, Year B, Year C.

> Vol. 2, Weekdays, Year 1, Proper of Saints, Common of Saints.

> Vol. 3, Weekdays, Year 2, Proper of Saints, Common of Saints.

> Vol. 4, Common of Saints, Ritual Masses, Masses for Various Needs, Votive Masses, Masses for the Dead.

National Conference of Catholic Bishops. Book of the Gospels for Use in the Dioceses of the United States of America. Second Typical Edition.

Revised Common Lectionary (Episcopal Edition). New York: Church Publishing, 2007.

Study Editions

Lectionary for Mass, Sundays, Solemnities, Feasts of the Lord and Saints, Study Edition. Chicago: Liturgy Training Publications, 1970, 1998.

The Weekday Lectionary: Study Edition. Chicago: Liturgy Training Publications, 2002.

Consultation on Common Texts. The Revised Common Lectionary. Abingdon Press, 1992.

Lectionary for Worship: Study Edition: Year A, Year B, Year C. Minneapolis: Augsburg Fortress, 2007, 2006, 2008. (Evangelical Lutheran Church in America.)

Resources for Lector Preparation and Study

Workbook for Lectors, Gospel Readers, and Proclaimers of the Word®. Chicago: Liturgy Training Publications, published annually.

Prendergast, Michael R., Susan E. Meyers, and Timothy M. Milinovich. *Pronunciation Guide for the Lectionary: A Comprehensive Resource for Proclaimers of the Word.* Chicago: Liturgy Training Publications, 2009.

Powell, Mark Allan et al. with the Society for Biblical Literature. *HarperCollins Bible Dictionary.* New York: HarperOne, 2011.

Brown, Raymond E., SS. *101 Questions and Answers on the Bible.* Mahwah, NJ: Paulist Press, 2003.

Frigge, Marielle, OSB. *Beginning Biblical Studies.* Winona, MN: Anselm Academic, 2013.

New Collegeville Bible Commentary Series. Collegeville, MN: Liturgical Press.

Liturgy and the Bible Series

Bergant, Dianne, CSA. *O Lord, Open My Lips: The Psalms in the Liturgy.* Chicago: Liturgy Training Publications, 2018.

Boisclair, Regina A. *The Word of the Lord at Mass: Understanding the Lectionary.* Chicago: Liturgy Training Publications, 2015.

Cameron, Michael. *Unfolding Sacred Scripture: How Catholics Read the Bible.* Chicago: Liturgy Training Publications, 2015.

Clifford, Richard J., SJ. *Thus Says the Lord: The Prophets in the Liturgy.* Chicago, Liturgy Training Publications, 2021.

Senior, Donald, CP. *Composing Sacred Scripture: How the Bible Was Formed.* Chicago: Liturgy Training Publications, 2016.

Resources for Prayer and Reflection

Casey, Michael. *Sacred Reading: The Ancient Art of Lectio Divina.* Liguori, MO: Liguori, 1997.

Magrassi, Mariano, OSB. *Praying the Bible: An Introduction to Lectio Divina.* Translated by Edward Hagman, OFM CAP. Collegeville, MN: Liturgical Press, 1998.

Shea, John. *The Spiritual Wisdom of the Gospels for Christian Preachers and Teachers.* Collegeville, MN: Liturgical Press:
Matthew, Year A: On Earth As It Is in Heaven, 2004.
Mark, Year B: Eating with the Bridegroom, 2005.
Luke, Year C: The Relentless Widow, 2006.
Feasts, Funerals, Weddings: Following Love into Mystery, 2010.

Websites

New American Bible, Revised Edition: www.usccb.org/bible.

Lectionary Readings: https://bible.usccb.org

Revised Common Lectionary: https://lectionary.library.vanderbilt.edu.

Resources from the World of Acting

Hagen, Uta, and Haskel Frankel. *Respect for Acting.* New York: Wiley, 1973.

Spolin, Viola. *Improvisation for the Theatre.* 3rd ed. Evanston, IL: Northwestern University Press, 1999.

Spolin, Viola, Paul Sills, and Carol Sills. *Theater Games for the Lone Actor.* Evanston, IL: Northwestern University Press, 2001.

Stanislavsky, Konstantin. *An Actor Prepares.* Trans. Elizabeth Reynolds Hapgood. New York: Theatre Arts, 1936.

Stanislavsky, Konstantin. *Building a Character.* Trans. Elizabeth Reynolds Hapgood. New York: Theatre Arts, 1949.

Stanislavsky, Konstantin. *Creating a Role.* Trans. Elizabeth Reynolds Hapgood. New York: Theatre Arts, 1961.